CALIFORNIA

VINES, WINES & PIONEERS

SHERRY MONAHAN

D1457161

AMERICAN PALATE

Published by American Palate
A Division of The History Press
Charleston, SC 29403
www.historypress.net

Copyright © 2013 by Sherry Monahan
All rights reserved

Cover images: *Front*: Italian Swiss Colony harvest wagon. *Courtesy of Asti Winery, Treasury Wine Estates*; Hall-Bergfeld Vineyards. *Courtesy of Hall Wines*. *Back*: Wente family, circa 1895. *Courtesy of Wente Vineyards*; Far Niente Vineyards. *Courtesy of Sherry Monahan*.

First published 2013

Manufactured in the United States

ISBN 978.1.60949.884.9

Library of Congress CIP data applied for.

To my husband Larry, V.2, for making dinners and everything else the spouse of a deadline-driven author does. To my friend Chris Enss, who despite downturns in life is rarely seen without a kind smile or a funny quip.

To all my family and friends who have always listened and supported me.

Thanks!

CONTENTS

FOREWORD

Reading through *California Vines, Wines & Pioneers* took me back to my childhood. Names of towns, streets, businesses, wineries and vineyards all sparked fond memories of growing up in Napa Valley. The people behind the names had little significance to me back then, but they have emerged over the decades as the bedrock of our industry. Author Sherry Monahan has written a thorough and intriguing account of California wine's founding fathers (and, more rarely, mothers). She has bridged the gap between these nineteenth-century visionaries and the omnipresent and international wine businesses of the twenty-first century whose seeds were, in fact, planted by those visionaries generations ago.

Ms. Monahan's story vividly captures the foresight and determination of these pioneers and the challenges they faced as they wrote the history of the Wild West. She also ferrets out the histories of our founding families, tracing them back to their homelands. The impressive role that Europe played in shaping this nascent California trade is worth noting. All of these wine pioneers came from the quintessential wine growing countries of Europe with their "Old World wines." She eloquently describes their arrival, some through very circuitous routes, and the journey to planting vines and vinifying their fruit. From eclectic backgrounds and of mostly modest means, they shared a determination to overcome anything in their way. For some, obstacles such as phylloxera and prohibition proved too daunting, but more often than not, failed endeavors were later reborn under new owners with new visions.

California Vines, Wines & Pioneers impressively chronicles the grape varieties that were planted at the dawn of our industry. These varieties were as varied as their owners' origins, but the common grape connecting many growers and vintners was Cabernet Sauvignon, a vestige of their Old World heritage. These nineteenth-century immigrants came full circle by shipping their wares back to the Old World, competing against their European counterparts and garnering prestigious awards in the process. History repeated itself with the Paris Tasting of 1976 when California wines again prevailed, as they often had the century before.

Sherry Monahan's stories, bolstered by her passion for genealogy and historical research, have broadened our knowledge of the founders and descendants of the California wine business. Stories have always been used to sell bottles of wine. We now have more stories, accurately told, that bring life to our industry. Her book celebrates the lives of the Old World settlers and the visionaries who shepherded the historic wineries and vineyards, and California wine, into the present.

This work adds a new dimension to the terroir that we taste in our wines today. Next time you enjoy a glass, toast our history. I know I will.

Salute,

Peter Mondavi Jr.
Co-proprietor, Charles Krug Winery

ACKNOWLEDGEMENTS

There are so many people I need to thank for helping me with this book. First, to my "wine" people, David and Jennifer Faircloth. While sampling some Seghesio wine in their shop, they told me about Edoardo's story, and that's when I got the idea to write this book. To The History Press and my commissioning editor, Aubrie Koenig, for accepting my idea. To my dear and nutty friend, author Chris Enss. Her tireless efforts to help me get endorsements and publicity for this book went beyond the call of friendship duty. To the wineries and their staff for taking the time to share their history, their family stories and their wine! Special thanks to Peter Mondavi Jr. of the Krug estate, Anna Miranda and the Count at Buena Vista, Joel Peterson at Ravenswood and James and John Concannon of Concannon Family Vineyards. Thanks also to these wineries: Bucklin, Edmeades, Far Niente, Foppiano Vineyards, Freemark Abbey, Frog's Leap, Fulton, Hall/Bergfeld, Inglenook, Korbel, Kunde, Langtry Estates, Nichelini, Saucelito Canyon, Schramsberg, Scott Harvey, Sebastiani, Seghesio, Trefethen, Valley of the Moon, V. Sattui and Wente. Special thanks to Harlan Hague for connecting me to Dana DiRicco and her husband, Glenn Benjamin, DVM, who gave me room and board in Lake County, and for connecting me to her friend Carole Mascherini. Carole and her husband, Gino Ballaghio, offered us a place to stay in Healdsburg that was nestled among Chardonnay vines.

Additional thanks to everyone who shared their winery or vineyard histories, family stories, wine samples, recipes, photographs and personal details. Having those things make this book more of a personal story rather than just straight facts. Most importantly: thanks for your time.

INTRODUCTION

Today, Napa, Sonoma and other Northern California regions are synonymous with California wine, but that wasn't always the case. It was the Franciscan missionaries sent over from Spain who planted the first grapes in Southern California. As they migrated north from Mexico, they set up missions beginning with San Diego in 1769 and ending with Sonoma in 1823, planting grapes along the way. They planted a grape called the mission grape or *criolla medina*.

By 1831, Los Angeles had blossomed into the largest grape growing region in California, and Hubert H. Bancroft noted that the city of Los Angeles had more than one hundred acres of vineyards, with nearly half of the 200,000 vineyards in the country. Some of the largest producers were the local missions. According to William Heath Davis, who arrived in California in 1831, Frenchman Jean Louis Vignes was the first man to establish a nonmission vineyard. Vignes is credited with being the first to introduce *Vitis vinifera* to California, which are cultivated European grapes. In his 1886 book *Sixty Years in California: A History of Events and Life in California*, Davis called Vignes "the father of the wine industry." He was also the first to plant and cultivate oranges in Los Angeles. The city of Los Angeles flourished as the California wine hub for several years, until a little discovery at Sutter's mill created an increased demand for local wine in mining areas.

California's population boomed when news of the gold rush broke in mid-1848 from Sutter's Camp in Coloma. By the end of 1849, some eighty thousand immigrants from France, Italy, China, Germany, Hungary and other countries had come to seize their dreams of a golden fortune. By 1852, many knew that their chance of realizing that dream was no closer than when they arrived.

By the 1850s, new viticultural areas like Sonoma, Napa, Sutter, Lake, Yuba, Butte, Trinity and El Dorado Counties were emerging. In 1857, Napa County reportedly made its first wine shipment to San Francisco, which consisted of six bottles and six casks.

Even though Northern California was using the mission grapes from the Franciscans, many new immigrants were used to wines from Europe. Historian Lyman L. Palmer wrote this in 1881 about mission wine: "It was sour, unpalatable and dreggy stuff, yet it answered the purpose, and was relished by those accustomed to its use from youth to old age…And again we are enjoying a glass of Mr. Krug's Sherry, Mr. Crabb's Angelica, Mr. Schram's Hock or Claret or in fact the pure, delicious wines that are produced at any of the cellars in Napa County." He noted that when Americans first came to the area, they were content to use the same grapes the missionaries used. But as time progressed, Californians sought a better wine, more like what they were used to from their native countries. In the 1850s, the *Southern Vineyard* noted, "The true policy of our wine makers is to make the best wine which the grapes of our soil, and the climate of our country will produce, without any regard to its peculiar aroma or flavor."

According to a report made by author E.N. Wallace in 1901:

> *It will probably always be a question, who was the first to introduce the foreign varieties of vines into California. It is known that a Mr. Stock of San Jose, had several varieties growing on his place as early as 1858, which he had received from his father, who resided in Germany. In 1861 Dr. Crane of St. Helena purchased cuttings from the Stock vineyard… There was one variety which had no label, and Mr. Stock sold them at half price, and they proved to be the now celebrated Riesling, and these cuttings were the first of that variety ever planted in Napa county…In 1861 Col. Haraszthy was appointed commissioner…to visit the wine growing countries of Europe…the result…was the importation of some three hundred different varieties of vines.*

In an 1860 report, winemaker Antoine Delmas recommended certain grapes to make specific wines. For reds, he suggested Balzac, Barbaroux, Black Burgundy, Black Cluster, Black Hamburg, Cabernet, Charbonneau Dischia Gris, Large Rosa of Peru, Malvoisie de Berlin, Meunier Noir and a few others. For whites, he recommended Blanc de Bergerac, Blanc Doux (white sweet), Gros Cadillac, Riesling and Tokay de Sunel. He also noted that these additional vines would do well for general cultivation in some locales: Black Malvoisie, Flame Colored Tokay, Royal Muscadine and Sweet Water.

With the planting of these new vines, California viticulture, which is the study of grape cultivation, entered a whole new realm. Men (and yes, a woman or two) planted vines and began bottling wine, and the winemaking industry flourished throughout the latter part of the 1800s. While today there appear to be as many wineries as there are vineyards, that wasn't the case early on. In fact, there were very few wineries making the wine but plenty of people growing grapes. The majority of people listed in the census records in the early to mid-1800s were recorded as farmers, wine growers or vineyardists. It was rare to see "winemaker" as an occupation. Another reason for many selling their grapes to bigger companies like Krug or Buena Vista was because the small vineyardists couldn't afford to construct and maintain a modern winery. The wine many made was not that good and helped give California's wine a "bad name" for a while. All that changed toward the turn of the century.

In 1875, California winemakers were producing more than 5 million gallons of wine, with about 1 million being shipped. Production increased each season, and between 4 and 7 million gallons were made over the next few years, despite an agricultural and industrial depression that hit the U.S. economy during this time.

As president of the California Board of State Viticultural Commission, Agoston Haraszthy's son, Arpad Haraszthy, gave his annual report in 1888. He stated that when he became president in 1880, there were about fifty thousand vines planted, of which 90 percent were foreign varieties. Wine production in 1880 was 10,200,000 gallons, of which 2,487,353 gallons were shipped. Wine production increased to 15,000,000 gallons for 1887, in part due to there being more vineyards. By 1888, the number of vineyards had tripled since 1880. Popular grapes at the time were Zinfandel (also known as Black St. Peters), Malvoisie, Cabernet and Petit Pinot.

The word "phylloxera" can send waves of panic through even the calmest of winemakers and growers. It did just that in the early 1870s. Grape growers replanted their vines on new rootstock in the 1880s. This tiny pest destroyed numerous vineyards.

Prohibition was another deadly word that nearly destroyed the wine industry. Despite phylloxera and prohibition, many wineries, like the vines themselves, survived, including Buena Vista, Concannon, Freemark Abbey, Fulton, Inglenook, Krug, Schramsberg, Simi and many others. It took the pioneering spirit of their tenacious founders and the devotion of their current owners to remain a part of California's viniculture.

Turn the pages of this book to discover the stories of the pioneers who headed to California's gold rush country. Most may not have found a single nugget, but they planted vines and turn their fruits into liquid gold.

I've strived to uncover and include as many historic wineries and vineyards as possible. If I missed some, it wasn't for lack of trying. Who knows, if there's a great deal more, then maybe there's a volume two on the horizon.

Not all wine can be drunk alone, so I've included recipes from the wineries to "pair" with their history. Cheers!

Chapter 1

SACRAMENTAL GOLD

C alifornia's wine history began with the Franciscan missionaries, who were sent by Spain in the mid- to late eighteenth century with a purpose of spreading Christian faith to the native people. As they established missions along the Camino Real, or Royal Trail, from San Diego to Sonoma, they planted Mexican grapes for sacramental use and trade. These black grapes were called criolla but became known as "missionary grapes" and were California's first real grapes planted for wine.

Franciscan fathers like Friar Jose Altimira, who founded the Mission San Francisco de Solano, spread Christianity to the natives while they busily engaged in trades. Solano was founded on July 4, 1823, and was the twenty-first mission in California. The natives, mostly not there by choice, tilled the land and planted numerous orchards and vineyards. Many lonely pioneers visited their missions, as they often functioned as hotels since there were none at the time. Pioneer Vincent Carosso visited the missions often and wrote of the Sonoma Mission, "[I] was very kindly received by the Padre, and drank as fine red California wine as I ever have since, manufactured at the Mission from grapes brought from the Mission of Santa Clara and San Jose."

Until the mid-1800s, the mission grape was the primary winemaking grape in California. As time progressed, mission grapes were used for brandy, table wine and Angelica, which was a fortified wine. Nineteenth-century historian Hubert Bancroft noted that the sweet, reddish-black mission grape in Los Angeles was referred to as the South Spanish stock. He also noted that the

Sonoma Mission, circa 1835. Mission San Francisco Solano was founded on July 4, 1823 (twenty-first in order), by Padre Jose Altimira. The mission is named for St. Francis Solano, missionary to the Peruvian Indians. The Indian name was thought to be Sonoma. *Courtesy of Library of Congress.*

black Sonoma was fruitier and yielded a lighter wine. While the mission grapes served as the sacramental wine for the missionaries, a completely different version of California wine would debut some fifty years later.

Ludwig Louis Salvator was the archduke of Austria and visited the area in the 1870s, writing this about mission grapes:

> *Among all the products of Los Angeles none, probably, is more important than the grape. The so-called mission grape was brought in by the fathers in 1770 and extensively raised by the Indians under this tutelage. This, presumably, was of the Malaga variety known as Vino Carlo. In Mexico, however, from where the first cuttings were imported, many of its salient characteristics were lost, and it no longer resembles the Malaga grape. Though only a fair wine can be made from it, the fathers gave it the preference since it was both hardy and a prolific bearer. Even now 75 per cent of the grapevines in California are hardy bearers. In shape it is perfectly round, being when fully developed about three-quarters of an inch in diameter. While ripening it is of a reddish-brown color; when*

fully ripe it is a beautiful black and full of sweet juice, but without aroma. This is a considerable detriment, not only in the preparation of wine, but also in its use as a table grape. Wine made from this sort of grape is quite strong, resembling Port and Sherry. In and about Los Angeles the mission grape is especially popular and it was not until 1853 that new varieties of grape, especially those from Europe, were imported. These have gradually taken the place of the old mission grape, such kinds as the Flaming Tokay, Rose of Peru, Black Morocco, Black Hamburg, and the White Muscat being highly favored.

Mission grapes were also planted at Sutter's Fort before the great gold rush took place. Native New Yorker John Bidwell sought his fortune in California in 1841 and journeyed west as part of the first migrant train going overland from Missouri to California. He found work at Fort Sutter and sided with Governor Micheltorena in the 1844 revolt, but he aided the Bear Flag rebels in 1846. After serving with John Fremont, he returned to Fort Sutter. Bidwell was among the first to find gold on Feather River and used his earnings to secure a grant north of Sacramento in 1849. He spent the rest of his life as a farmer at "Rancho Chico" and became a leader of the state's agricultural interests. He claimed that

California is emphatically the land of the vine; and can there be any doubt that we can produce the finest wines? This is an important question, because we are actually importing in casks, barrels, baskets and cases, millions of gallons every year. And yet it is admitted that there is not a land beneath the sun better suited to grape culture than California. The name of Los Angeles is as famous for wine and for the grape as that of California for gold. But the grape flourishes well everywhere, and its cultivation is being extended all over the State.

Pioneer Heinrich Lienhard recalled his first trip to gold rush country:

On the seventh of January, 1848, Sutter and I rode out on horseback to inspect the property he had selected. It was situated in a country where the summers are unusually dry, near a broad, deep slough that was separated from the mouth of the American Fork by a kind of island, and proved to be an excellent site for a garden. When the tide was high, the American River over-flowed into this slough, which was deep enough to hold an ample supply of water for our garden during the dry months...For two or three weeks Sutter had been acting queerly. One day I had some business to transact in the fort; since it was noon I stayed there for dinner, and as I was leaving, he brought out a dirty old rag in which something was tied. He unfastened the knot, and showed us eighteen or twenty small pieces of metal, the largest about the size of a pinhead. These small grains were yellow and we began to think they might be gold.

The man who discovered the gold was an employee of General John A. Sutter named James W. Marshall. New Jersey native Marshall was working in Coloma for Sutter when he suddenly appeared at Sutter's home with a small item wrapped in a cloth. His secretive manner caused Sutter some concern, but Sutter abided by Marshall's wishes and met behind closed doors in Sutter's home. What Sutter saw would change California's history forever. Gold was discovered in 1848, and it lasted for four short years, with the last two seeing the supply dwindle to nothing more than dust.

That year, 100,000 miners earned an average $600 per year, despite wages for common labor being two to three times higher. The gold rush ended almost as quickly as it began, which left thousands of immigrants within a few years with no fortune and no job. A portion of them followed the next big mining circuit in America, which at the time was in Colorado, and some sailed back to their native countries; others still stayed and found employment. With California's burgeoning population, many found new occupations, including farming, grape growing and winemaking, which they had known in their own countries.

J.G. Player-Frowd was an Englishman who visited California in the early 1870s and observed, "The early wines of California were all falsified being mixed with strong foreign wines. The Los Angeles wine was not good enough to send out in

Major John August Sutter, 1859. Sutter wrote, "It was in the first part of January, 1848, when the gold was discovered at Coloma, where I was then building a saw-mill. The contractor and builder of this mill was James W. Marshall, from New Jersey." *Courtesy of Library of Congress.*

Barroom in the mines, circa 1850. Once news of the gold discovery was out, people descended on the area near Sutter's Fort. Basic staples, including wine, were far from cheap. According to gold rush pioneer Jacques Antoine Moerenhout, a bottle of "ordinary wine" or brandy sold for eight dollars, and the price of placer gold was paying sixteen dollars per ounce. *Courtesy of Library of Congress.*

its natural state, so the dealers doctored it, and these compounds went by the name of California wine, bringing no credit to the country. Meanwhile it was found that the mining towns in the mountains grew better grapes than the old Missions, and that the valleys of the coast range made better wine than any." He considered the "four great wine-growing districts" to be "Sonoma Valley, Napa Valley, Los Angeles, and Eldorado."

Chapter 2

NAPA PIONEERS

North Carolina native George C. Yount was the first white pioneer to arrive in the area by 1831, and in 1836, General Mariano Guadalupe Vallejo granted him the 11,814-acre Caymus Rancho. Two years later, he planted the first vines in Napa. A few years later, Rancho La Jota was also granted to Yount, and he surveyed the town of Yountville, which was named after him.

Today, Napa Valley is home to numerous outstanding wineries and vineyards, but before pioneers like Yount moved to the area, it was home to the Caymus Indians and numerous grizzly bears, which were known to frequent the area. Frank Leach was an early pioneer and newspaperman who recalled of Napa in the early days, "Napa Valley was early recognized as a section favorable for the growing of fruit, and a few enterprising farmers gave their attention to that business. Wells and Ralph Kilburn were among the pioneers. A man named Osborne planted the Zinfandel Oak Knoll orchard, and Captain Thompson the Suscol orchard, both of which became famous throughout the state before 1860. As is generally known, Napa in later years became noted as the largest wine growing district in the state."

He continued:

> *Orchards and wheat fields disappeared, being replaced by vineyards which for a time gave great profit to the owners, which probably was the cause of the overdoing of the business, placing the producers at the mercy of speculators…The first vineyard for wine making purposes was planted in*

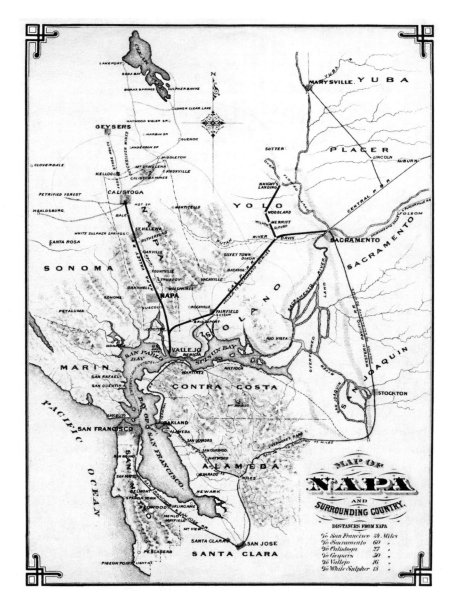

Napa area map, circa late 1800s. L. Vernon Briggs visited Napa in 1881 and recalled, "To the visitor at Napa City today, the statement that a little more than thirty years ago the site of the now lively little city was a 'howling wilderness' sounds more like a fable than a reality; and yet such is the case. It is situated in the midst of a country noted for its mild and genial climate, the great fertility of its soil, and its many well-cultivated vineyards. Those in Napa Valley produced in one year over twenty-six hundred thousand gallons of wine and brandy. This production was from sixty-one cellars." *Courtesy of Charles Krug Winery.*

the latter part of the '50s by John Patchett on a piece of land about a mile north-westerly from the courthouse in the town of Napa. Here the first wine on any scale was made. Doctor Crane, a physician in Napa, a very intelligent and observing man, had become thoroughly impressed with the idea that the soils and climate of Napa Valley were particularly favorable to the culture of the grape for wine purposes. As early as 1857, he contributed column after column to the pages of the local paper, giving his reasons therefor and urging the planting of vineyards, calling attention to the possibilities of the poorer lands, useless for the growing of grain. The doctor kept up his publications for two or three years, or it may be longer, until he finally gave up his practice and bought a brushy and gravel covered piece of land near the town of St. Helena not considered worth fencing and planted the vineyard that subsequently became famous.

While Yount both established a community and was a viticulturist, David Fulton was an inventor who focused on wine. After nearly two years of making saddles, horse-drawn carts and cast-iron parts, Fulton established his own vineyard by purchasing a forty-acre parcel of land from Frank Stratton on January 12, 1860. In the spring of that year, he planted about six acres of grapevines. The next year, anticipating more mature harvests to come, he sold fifteen of his undeveloped acres to finance his forty-eight- by twenty-eight-foot stone wine cellar. Fulton hired Anton Rossi of Spring Valley, and together they hauled one thousand square yards of dirt and moved in one hundred square yards of rhyolite rock quarried from the valley's eastern hillsides to build the cellar walls. Rossi was a native of Switzerland and arrived in America in 1871. By 1901, he had established his own winery.

The winery itself was a board-and-batten structure made of redwood planks milled from trees taken in the western hillsides. By May 1865, he was making and selling brandy. On August 7, 1869, Fulton was appointed to a committee of seven vintners at a California Agriculture Convention. Fulton was also a businessman, benefactor, trustee, inventor and town visionary. In 1870, utilizing skills as a blacksmith and the knowledge gained as owner of the town saddler, he invented the Fulton plow. David Fulton died in the fall of 1871, just two weeks before the grape harvest. The operation was left in the hands of David's wife, Mary Albino (Lyon) Fulton. In January 1876, she hired winemaker William Scheffler to take the helm. Mr. Scheffler worked for a year and a half retooling the old wine cellar. Scheffler was able to bring production up to current standards by the fall of 1877, doing so with enough momentum to carry the operation

David Fulton, circa mid-1800s. David was one of the first, if not the first, to plant vines in Napa. Today, their vineyards, originally planted in 1860, produce fewer than four hundred cases of Petite Sirah a year from their dry-farmed estate vineyard, which has been continuously family owned and operated. *Courtesy of David Fulton Winery.*

into the next decade as the M.A. Fulton Winery. Mary's health began to fail, and the Fultons decided to abandon commercial winemaking and concentrate solely on the vineyard during the 1880s.

Mary's two daughters, Ida and Alice, were given the ranch when Mary died in 1893, and Ida continued to live on the ranch and eventually acquired her sister's share of the property. Ida married Edgar Washington Mather in 1897, and the two expanded the vineyard acreage, erected a barn and built a tank house that stands today next to the 1864 farmhouse. Around the turn of the century, Edgar and Ida Mather bore three children: twins Edgar and Fulton and Gladys. With Edgar and Ida gone by the start of the 1930s, the property went to their three children. Shortly after, the brothers Edgar and Fulton gave their ownership of the farmhouse and vineyard to their sister. Gladys Mather married Ferdinand Wallace Beard, and the couple had a son named Edgar Darrel Beard and also took in Gladys's nephew, Fulton I. Mather Jr.

Both Edgar and Fulton worked in the vineyard, and several years later, when Gladys passed away, she gave a small portion of the St. Helena property

David Fulton's widow, Mary Albina Lyon Fulton, with her two daughters, Alice (left) and Ida (right), in about 1889. Ida is the daughter who married David Fulton Winery's current owner's grandfather, Edgar Washington Mather. *Courtesy of David Fulton Winery.*

to her grandson, Ed Beard Jr., while her son received their Yountville properties. The remainder of the St. Helena property went to Fulton I. Mather. Together with his wife, Erma L. Mather, they are current owners of the David Fulton Winery. Today, they produce less than four hundred cases of Petite Sirah a year from their 1860 dry-farmed estate vineyard.

Charles Krug began his winery around the same time as Fulton. He was born in Prussia in 1825, and Krug fought for independence from Germany in 1848. He was even jailed for his activism, yet he was freed nine months later in a second uprising. When the Prussian immigrant arrived in San Francisco in 1852, he had little besides willpower and a willingness to work hard. He became a major local winery figure of his era, greatly influencing Napa Valley's development as a world-renowned wine producing region.

Within months of Agoston Haraszthy's purchase of Buena Vista, Krug had located to Sonoma as well. However, there was something special about the Napa area, and two years later, Krug sold his small vineyard and move

Charles Krug, circa
late 1800s. The *Pacific
Wine and Spirit Review*
in 1892 wrote of Kurg,
"In person, Mr. Krug is
rather below the medium
height, but he has a trim
active figure and scarcely
looks fifty." *Courtesy of
Charles Krug Winery.*

to Napa Valley. In 1858, he borrowed an apple press and made wine in Napa
for pioneer John Patchett. A portion of his memoir appeared in the *Star* on
December 19, 1890:

> *When I first visited Napa county, I found less than a dozen small vineyards
> of so-called Mission vines…In October, 1858 I made the first lot of wine
> ever made in Napa county, at the place of John Patchett, Napa City. As
> a cellar, he used an old pioneer adobe house built on the banks of Napa
> creek. I said, "the first lot of wine ever made in Napa county." Allow me
> to correct this statement: they offered me in the Fall of 1859 at each of the
> Bale and Young ranchos, a tincup of "elegant" claret, which was fermented*

in large cowhides, tied to spread and with lassoes between four trees and filled with grapes crushed by Indians.

Once he arrived in Napa, he settled down and married Caroline Bale, whose father, Dr. Edwin Bale, was granted more than ten thousand acres in the area. On December 26, 1860, they were married. The couple had five children: Linda, Charles, Anita, Lolita and Karl.

In 1861, he founded his own winery and built a fourteen-foot-high by twenty-feet-deep cellar with a thatched roof. It was located one mile north of the town of St. Helena and was replaced by a more substantial structure several years later. His leadership was said to be inspirational and his ideas innovative. Charles Krug introduced the cider press for winemaking, the first of which is still on display at the winery. He carefully selected rootstocks, varietals and vineyard sites, which was a novel concept in late nineteenth-century America.

By 1868, Krug had 41,000 of the 1 million vines planted in Napa County, which made him the fourth-largest grower behind Samuel Brannon, Dr. Beldon Crane and the Siegrist brothers. By 1872, Krug's cellar building had grown to be 90 by 104 feet and held nearly 300,000 gallons. Krug grew Rieslings, Muscatel, Burger, Chasselas, Malaga, Black Malvoisie, Flame Tokay, Rose de Peru and Zinfandel. In 1874, a fire destroyed the winery, but a new cellar of stone, concrete and wood was built in August 1874. By the fall of 1880, Krug has expanded his cellar to a capacity of 700,000 gallons of wine.

In 1880, he began representing the Napa district as treasurer of the California Board of State Viticultural Commission, serving for ten years. In his annual report in 1882, he wrote, "It seems to me not improper to state that only fine varieties of grapes for wine making were planted, the leading variety being Zinfandel, 1,400 acres, followed by Gutedel (Chasselas), Riesling. Of Sauvignon, Chauche Gris, Burgundy, Charbono [*sic*], Mataro, Trousseau, and Pinot." It was also at the time when Krug began hosting people to sample his wine. According to a July 28, 1882 *Star* report, "On Monday evening a number of gentlemen…were invited to inspect the gas machines, its appliances, and the illuminating powers of the gas lately put into Krug's cellar…on arrival at the cellar, the sales selection which is something over one hundred feet in length and perhaps thirty in breadth, was found to be brilliantly lighted but with six jets, the light being very penetrating, yet mellow." Krug was also innovative when it came to grape growing, and in 1886, he began tying his vines to wire to train them. That same year, Krug

Krug winery employees, circa 1870s. In 1882, Krug reported, "It seems to me not improper to state here that only fine varieties of grapes for winemaking were planted, the leading variety being, Zinfandel, 1,400 acres, followed by Gutedel (Chasselas), and Riesling. Of Sauvignon, Chauche Gris, Burgundy, Charbono, Mataro, Trousseau, and Pinot." *Courtesy of Charles Krug Winery.*

took second place in the Cabernet Sauvignon category, and in 1887, he took first place for his Burgundy, Cabernet Sauvignon and his mixed Zinfandel. At the 1889 World's Fair in Paris, he won a bronze medal for his wine, but no record exists as to the category.

In 1892, after the phylloxera damage, census takers were sent to assess the extent of it. They noted that the Krug estate in St. Helena only had seventy-five acres, of which thirty-five were bearing fruit. He stated he was replanting five to ten acres to Riparia, thirty acres to Lenoir and five acres to Mondeuse, Cabernet Sauvignon, Burger, Cabernet Franc and other grafts. After his death in November 1892, James Moffitt held the winery in proprietorship through prohibition. By 1943, he had found a pioneering spirit in Cesare Mondavi, an Italian immigrant with a passion for wine, and sold the winery to his family for $75,000. At sixty years old, Cesare Mondavi spearheaded a dramatic renaissance in the decade that followed. Cesare died in 1959, leaving wife Rosa as president, with sons Robert as general manager and Peter as vice-president. In 1966, Robert moved south to Oakville and began construction of his own winery. Upon Rosa's death in 1976, Peter became president of the winery. Today, the Mondavi family makes two wines with historical significance. Their Napa Valley Cabernet Sauvignon Stone Man is a tribute to Charles Krug because, as the Mondavis say, "[as a] revolutionary, activist and entrepreneur, he earned the reputation as a man of stone—strong, timeless, enduring…We invite you to enjoy our Stone Man Cabernet Sauvignon, a wine worthy of honoring Charles Krug and one that shares many of his best characteristics." The other is their Vintage Selection Cabernet Sauvignon, which the Mondavi family has been making since 1944.

Jacob Schram was born in May 1826 in the small town of Pfeddersheim, Germany, along the Rhine River, He came from a winemaking family, and when he was sixteen, Schram immigrated to New York. He was educated in the trade of barbering, and in 1852, he sailed across the Caribbean, crossed over the Panama Isthmus and continued up to San Francisco. He spent the next several years barbering, eventually moving his way north to the Napa Valley.

In 1859, he married Annie Christine Weaver, also from Germany. They started a family, and for several years, Jacob continued to barber full time. He turned to his winemaking heritage in 1862 when he purchased a large piece of land on the mountainsides of Napa Valley. They cleared the wooded and wild land and built a rustic cabin to shelter them from the weather. They also planted European varietals and began to produce wine.

Jacob remained a barber to supplement his income while the work at Schramsberg continued. After fully realizing the summer heat in the area, he hired Chinese workers to help him dig his cool underground cellars. Annie was often left in charge of the hired hands as Jacob visited fellow vintners in the valley and took on the role of salesman both near and far. By 1876, his production was up to twelve thousand gallons. From this small start, the winery and vineyards continued to grow until they had fifty acres of bearing vines and were producing upward of twelve thousand cases per year.

Jacob shipped his Riesling, Hock, Burgundy and Chasselas to New York and beyond. His wines were winning awards at American and international competitions. As they continued to prosper, the Schrams had a lavish Victorian residence built to replace the original cabin. A shipbuilder and his team were hired for the construction, and small pegs were used in place of the more modern nail. The house became a gathering spot for the many friends and colleagues with whom the Schrams had become familiar. The Schram house is still lived in to this day, and it retains its spirit of hospitality.

Jacob Schram with the Beringer brothers. Robert Louis Stevens wrote of Schram, "Mr. Schram's, on the other hand, is the oldest vineyard in the valley—eighteen years old, I think; yet he began a penniless barber, and even after he had broken ground up here with his Black Malvoisies, continued for long to tramp the valley with his razor. Now, his place is the picture of prosperity; stuffed birds in the veranda, cellars far dug into the hill-side, and resting on pillars like a bandit's cave—all trimness, varnish, flowers, and sunshine, among the tangled wildwood." *Courtesy of Schramsberg Winery.*

Annie Schram at entrance to caves. Robert Louis Stevens recalled of Annie: "Stout, smiling Mrs. Schram, who has been to Europe and apparently all about the States for pleasure, entertained Fanny in the veranda while I was tasting wines in the cellar." *Courtesy of Schramsberg Winery.*

PALACE HOTEL WINES.

PURE CALIFORNIA WINES—DIRECT FROM VINEYARD.

ORLEANS VINEYARD.	PTS.	QTS.	HEDGESIDE VINEYARD.	PTS.	QTS.
Eclipse, Ext. Dry (Champagne) ...$1 25		$2 25	Cabernet (Claret)..........................$ 50		$1 00
Zinfandel (Claret)........................	30	50	Sauterne	50	1 00
Riesling (Hock)	30	50	SCHRAMSBERG		
			Riesling (Hock)	40	75
NAPA VALLEY WINE CO.			INGLENOOK VINEYARD		
Zinfandel	30	50	Zinfandel	40	75
			SUNNY SLOPE VINEYARD.		
BARTON VINEYARD.			Sherry....................................		1 00
Riesling...................................	30	50	Port......................................		1 00

Also San Gabriel Wine Co. Wines.

CHAMPAGNES.

	PTS	QTS		PTS	QTS
Dry Monopole, Heidsieck & Co.............	2 00	4 00	Pommery, Sec $2 00		$4 00
Gold Lack, Sec...........................	2 00		Krug, Sec 2 00		4 00
L. Roederer, Carte Blanche...............	2 00	4 00	Charles Heidsieck......................		3 50
Perrier, Jouet, Extra Dry,................	2 00		Sparkling Johannisberger................		3 50
Jules Mumm & Co., Grand Sec.............		4 00	G. H. Mumm & Co., Extra Dry........... 2 00		
Moet & Chandon.........................	2 00		Veuve Clicquot Ponsardin, Dry........... 2 00		4 00

CLARETS.

St. Julien, Pouget Fils.....................$ 50		$1 00	Chateau Lafitte, Dubos Freres..............		$4 00
St. Julien, Barton & Guestier, ...	75	1 50	Chateau Pavell Margaux, A. De Luze & Fils.		3 00
Chateau Leoville, A. De Luze & Fils...... 1 25		2 50	Chateau Leoville, 1874, Barton & Guestier..		4 00

This 1889 Palace Hotel menu shows Jacob Schram's wine on the menu of the Palace Hotel. It was one of a few California wines to make the menu for several years. *Courtesy of Schramsberg Winery.*

In the fall of 1900, Annie was stricken with paralysis, and she went steadily downhill until she died in the summer of 1901. The seventy-five-year-old Jacob continued running the business with his son, Herman, until the spring of 1905, when he took ill. He quickly worsened and died. The *St. Helena Star* noted, "His funeral was largely attended and extended the length of Spring Street, and his body was laid to rest beside his wife Annie in the marble city." Although Herman attempted to continue the business, phylloxera and prohibition brought an end to the Schram era.

Herman sold the property to Sterling Investment Company, which in 1916 sold it to a wealthy San Francisco contractor, W.J. McKillop, for use as a summer home. He later sold it to Captain Raymond C. Naylor. Following him was John Gargano, who purchased the property in 1940 and was a mysterious character somehow connected to bootlegging activity. In 1951, Gargano sold the property to Douglas Pringle.

Mrs. Pringle was the legendary grande dame Katharine Cebrian. In 1957, the winery was named a state historical landmark. The Pringles threw a lavish party with movie stars and glamorous girls circulating throughout a crowd of more than five hundred people. Katherine Cebrian divorced Douglas Pringle in 1959 and moved back to San Francisco. She sold the property

The Schram family. According to Robert Louis Stevens, "So local, so quintessential is a wine, that it seems the very birds in the veranda might communicate a flavor, and that romantic cellar influence the bottle next to be uncorked in London, and the smile of jolly Mr. Schram might mantle in the glass." *Courtesy of Schramsberg Winery.*

to Jack and Jamie Davies in 1965. Thus Schramsberg entered the modern era. Today, the winery makes sparkling wine under the Schramsberg label, Pinot Noir under the Davies Vineyards label and its estate-grown Cabernet Sauvignon under the J. Davies label.

While Peter Mondavi and his sons carry on the heritage of Charles Krug, Robert Mondavi does the same for pioneer Hamilton W. Crabb. Hamilton was one of those pioneers who came to California to search for gold, albeit a little late. He arrived in January 1853 and immediately set out for the mines. He worked in Placer and Nevada Counties for six months before heading to Alameda County. By 1860, Hamilton had married his first wife, Rebecca, and had two children named Amanda and Ada. In 1865, he moved to Napa County and started off in the grape business. In January 1868, H.W. Crabb purchased 240 acres in Oakville and named it Hermosa Vineyards. Crabb, who was born in Ohio on New Year's Day in 1828, immediately began planting several varietals. In 1880, his production was 300,000 gallons of wine. In May 1880, he sold several of his cuttings, including Zinfandel, Black Malvoisie, Chasselas, Burgundy, Berger, Johannesburg Riesling, Muscat and

Mataro. He acquired more land and named his ranch To Kalon, which is Greek for "the highest beauty." He began distilling in 1878 and gradually increased his brandy production from 2,201 gallons to 4,338 gallons in 1881. The Tokay and Muscat were used for "table purposes," while the others were used for wine and brandy.

Two of Crabb's wines received attention from the St. Helena Grower's Association in 1882 when they were introduced. Samples of his Elvira and Lenoir grapes were presented. Some commented favorably, saying, "The former is a white wine with a Catawba flavor, the latter a red—almost black—and full-bodied claret. They were tasted by the gentlemen present, who found them nice wines." Because he had more than two hundred varieties by 1883, state viticultural commissioner Charles Wetmore tried to settle confusion of the various names of the vines. He said, "For instance, the names Pinot and Chasselas refer to classes, and not a single variety of wine, there being about forty varieties of the Chasselas alone." Hamilton died at the age of seventy-one in early March 1899 and was mistakenly identified as Henry W. in his death announcement. By 1978, Robert Mondavi had acquired 250 acres of Crabb's original 359-acre vineyard, including some of the oldest Cabernet Sauvignon vines in the Napa Valley and what some believe to be the oldest Sauvignon Blanc vines in the western hemisphere. Today, the Robert Mondavi Winery's To Kalon Vineyard encompasses 550 acres.

Jacob Beringer left his home in Mainz, Germany, in 1868 to start a new life in the United States. He was enticed by his brother, Frederick, who had sailed to New York five years earlier and constantly wrote home about the grand opportunities in the vast new world. New York did not appeal to Jacob, however. He had enjoyed working in wine cellars in Germany when he was younger and had heard that the warm, sunny climate of California was ideal for growing wine grapes. In 1870, then, he traveled by train from the East Coast, first to San Francisco and then on to Napa Valley. Upon his arrival, he discovered rocky, well-drained soils similar to those in his native Rhine Valley.

The volcanic soil was ideal for growing the same grapes found in Europe's great winemaking regions. Best of all, the hills could be dug out to provide storage and aging tunnels that would maintain the constant temperature needed to produce fine wines. Jacob (who worked as winery foreman for Charles Krug) and his brother, Frederick, bought 215 acres on September 3, 1875, for $14,500 and set about making wines that compared to the best

Jacob Louis Beringer, circa 1800s. Jacob was born in May 1845 in Germany and married his Austrian wife, Agnes, in 1880. The couple had six children, with Jacob Jr. being the first. *Courtesy of Beringer Winery.*

Frederick Beringer, circa 1800s. Frederick, who came to America first, was born in January 1840. He married New York native Bertha in 1868, and they had three children. Frederick went by the nickname "Fritz." *Courtesy of Beringer Winery.*

in Europe; in 1876, they founded the Beringer Brothers Winery. The purchase included a two-story farmhouse (the current Hudson House) and a 28-acre vineyard that was already planted with White Riesling, Chappelt and Cabernet Sauvignon. The year 1876 was their first harvest, and they crushed forty thousand gallons of wine. Their stone gravity-flow winery was completed in 1877, and in about 1880, Jacob left Krug to work full time at his winery.

The tough task of hand-chiseling the tunnels in the mountainside behind the winery fell to Chinese workers who had returned to the Bay Area after helping build the Transcontinental Railroad. The tunnels took several years to complete but were the perfect place to age and store fine wine. While the winery was being built, Jacob took up residence in a farmhouse on the property built in 1848, now referred to as the Hudson House. It's been meticulously restored and expanded and serves as Beringer Vineyards' Culinary Arts Center.

In 1883, Frederick permanently moved to the Napa Valley and began construction of a seventeen-room mansion that was to be his home, a recreation of the Beringer family home on the Rhine River in Germany. The Rhine House is the center of Beringer's reserve and library tastings. It's a place where guests can enjoy a glass of wine while relaxing in the old library or on the same porch where Frederick once sat, overlooking the expansive lawns, lush gardens and out across the Napa Valley. An 1888 *Napa Journal* article noted, "Beringer Bros. have withdrawn 250 barrels of grape brandy from the bonded warehouse for export to Bremen, to be shipped from San Francisco by the Clipper ship Deutschland. They have also withdrawn from the Santa Rosa warehouse the same amount for the same place."

While the winery business was going well, Frederick suffered with Bright's disease. After a long battle with his illness, he passed away at his St. Helena home in 1901. His widow, Bertha, sold their shares of the winery to Jacob to continue the winery operations. Just five years later, Jacob died.

In 1918, when prohibition was enacted, two hundred acres of vineyards were farmed, and Beringer continued annual production of about fifteen thousand cases of "altar" wines until 1933, when prohibition was repealed. Varieties grown were Sauvignon Vert, Johannisberg Riesling, Cabernet Sauvignon, Petite Sirah, Alicante, Golden Chasselas, Semillon, Gutedel, Green Hungarian and Burger. Also during prohibition, Beringer found a niche of shipping dried wine grapes, which would help them survive the next decade. In 1934, Beringer Brothers opened its doors to the public for guided tours and sales.

Inglenook Vineyard was founded in 1879 by Finnish captain Gustave Niebaum, who used his enormous wealth to import the best European grapevines to Napa. In 1868, Gustave sailed into San Francisco's harbor with a ship loaded with Alaskan furs. He created the Alaska Commercial Company and, during a fifty-year span, built important trading stations in the Yukon and Aleutian Islands. The company also owned ocean steamers, sailing vessels and riverboats, which were the only means of transportation to and from San Francisco during the gold rush, as well as fur operations and salmon canneries.

In 1872, William C Watson, son-in-law of George C. Yount and manager of the Bank of Napa, bought the 78-acre G. Koni farm, west of Rutherford. He named it Inglenook, which is a Scottish expression meaning "cozy corner" or "fireside," and planted the first vines. In 1879, William Watson sold Inglenook to Judge S. Clinton Hastings, who founded the University of California Hastings Law School. Hastings quickly sold the 78 acres to Niebaum that same year. By this time, Niebaum had amassed a personal fortune in excess of $10 million and purchased a 440-acre farm from Mrs. Rohlwing. The total cost of both farms was $48,000. It's interesting to note that Niebaum originally intended to build a winery in Europe, but his new wife didn't share her husband's love of the sea and insisted that they stay in the San Francisco area.

Hamden W. McIntyre, an agent of the Alaska Commercial Company, was appointed general manager of Inglenook in 1881. Niebaum then commissioned William Mooser, a San Francisco architect, to design the chateau in conjunction with McIntyre, who provided the winery design. Niebaum then traveled to Europe to buy rootstock in Bordeaux, France. In 1882, he planted the first Merlot vines in Napa Valley, along with Cabernet Sauvignon. His first vintage in 1882 consisted of eight thousand gallons and was produced in makeshift cellar on the back of the property. During this process, Niebaum distinguished himself from other growers by sorting all his grapes and separating them from field debris before they were crushed. He also added an additional 712 acres from five neighboring estates, and he and McIntyre dug a small cellar into the hillside behind the mansion to test their theory of cellar temperatures and construction.

In 1883, construction of Inglenook Chateau began, and from 1883 to 1889, Niebaum worked with the Board of State Viticulture Commissioners to attempt to eradicate phylloxera. In 1884, Inglenook increased its capacity from 80,000 gallons to 125,000 gallons, and in 1886, a full line of Inglenook wines were presented at a meeting of the Wine and Spirit Traders' Society of New York. They were the nation's leading spirit importers, and when the testing was complete, Inglenook wines were judged the best California wines ever to have been shown there. The Inglenook Chateau, built into a hill, was completed in 1888. It was built as a gravity-flow winery, and grapes were loaded on the third floor before flowing into large redwood fermenters on the second floor and then finally into large casks on the ground floor.

One year later, Niebaum pioneered the first sterile bottling line in the Napa Valley to protect the reputation of his wines. His bottles, which bore the Inglenook label, were also wrapped in wire mesh and featured a tamper-proof lead seal in the punt. After only ten years, Niebaum's goal of producing a California wine "to equal and excel the most famous vintages of Europe" was on the brink of realization. His attention to detail and extreme hygiene in the winery attracted the attention of winemakers and journalists, and the *San Francisco Chronicle* devoted a two-page feature on Niebaum's pioneering methods.

The 1901 Inglenook wines were being served on ships in the South Pacific and in dining cars of the Southern Pacific Railroad. Seven years later, Captain Gustave Niebaum died on August 5, 1908, at the age of sixty-six, as a result of heart disease. Inglenook remained closed for three years until John Daniel Sr. and his family moved to Inglenook to help Mrs. Niebaum reopen the winery. Daniel was the husband of Mrs. Niebaum's niece, Leah. When Leah died from diphtheria in 1914, Daniel turned to her aunt, Mrs. Niebaum, to help bring up his children, Susanne and John Daniel Jr. One year later, Inglenook wine triumphed by winning nineteen gold medals at San Francisco's Panama Pacific International Exhibition, which celebrated the opening of the Panama Canal.

When prohibition was enacted in 1919, Mrs. Niebaum decided to sell Inglenook's grapes to neighboring Beaulieu Vineyard, which was making wines for religious and medicinal purposes, thus saving Inglenook. When prohibition was repealed on December 5, Inglenook hosted an all-day celebration the next day for three hundred guests. Mrs. Niebaum appointed expert winemaker Carl Bundschu as director of Inglenook, and he reaffirmed Inglenook's adherence to its traditionally high standards. The next year, John Daniel Jr. graduated from Stanford University with an engineering degree, but he gave up his dream of being a pilot to join the family estate and work alongside Bundschu to learn about the wine business. In 1934, Inglenook won first place for its Claret at the California State Fair. Two years later, Mrs. Niebaum died, and John Daniel Jr. and his sister, Susanne, inherited the estate. Susanne moved south to create a horse ranch, while John continued the family legacy. By 1939, John's meticulous management of Inglenook had become famous throughout the world. Inglenook received the largest number of awards of any California winery at the Golden Gate International Exposition in San Francisco. Inglenook also played host to many Hollywood stars, including Clark Gable and Jean Harlow.

At its 1954 Diamond Jubilee, John used the slogan "Pride, Not Profit" in his advertisements, which was fitting because, like his uncle Gustave, he was subsidizing winery operations from his personal wealth. The uncompromising management of the Inglenook estate installed by Niebaum and continued under John's stewardship started to take its toll. In 1964, the winery turned eighty-five years old and was in need of costly repairs and new equipment. The winemaker talked of retiring, and John Daniel Jr. was nearing sixty. With all that on his plate, he decided to sell Inglenook to Allied Grape Growers.

The purchase included the Inglenook name, the chateau and 94 acres of land, of which seventy-two were planted vineyards, facing Highway 29. Later that year, United Vintners was formed, and it officially owned Inglenook. John retained the Niebaum mansion and the surrounding 1,500 acres to the back of the Inglenook estate, where he and his family continued to live. Sadly, he could no longer use the Inglenook name or the chateau image. In 1965, the new corporate owners streamlined the production process, despite their promise to John Daniel. With so many changes to his family winery, he became disenchanted with the industry. After his death in 1970, his wife was convinced that winemaking was not a suitable career for her two daughters and sold the mansion and the remainder of the estate.

The timing was almost perfect for legendary film director Francis Ford Coppola, who was searching for a small family weekend property. During his visit, he fell in love with the natural beauty of the "back property." Much to his dismay, the fixed bid auction rapidly put him out of the running, but in 1976, he and his wife, Eleanor, successfully purchased 1,560 acres of the Inglenook estate with the proceeds from his *Godfather* films. Two years later, the first harvest of Niebaum-Coppola's wine—which was a Bordeaux-style blend of Cabernet Sauvignon, Cabernet Franc and Merlot—was made. Ironically, it was made in the cellars of the original winery on the back property where Niebaum first made his wine. In 1995, the Coppolas purchased the vineyards to the front of the property and the historic chateau with the profits from his movie *Bram Stoker's Dracula*. This purchase reunited the estate and its chateau for the first time in three decades. One year later, Coppola acquired the Gustave Niebaum Commemorative Series brand and redesigned the label to bring back the Black Label Claret, which was one of Niebaum's original wines. In 2002, he purchased vineyards from part of the adjoining J.J. Cohn property, located on the southern edge of the estate, and winemaking returned to the chateau after thirty-six years. The following year, Coppola realized Niebaum's dream by successfully carving cellars under the hill behind the chateau.

Gustave Niebaum, 1880. Gustave Ferdinand Nybom was born in Helsinki, Finland, on August 30, 1842. In 1861, he graduated from the Nautical Institute in Helsinki, and at the age of twenty-two, he commanded a ship headed to Alaska, which was part of the Russian empire. *Courtesy of Inglenook Winery.*

Niebaum Winery workers, circa late 1800s. In 1873, Gustave changed his last name to "Niebaum" and married Pennsylvania native Susanne Shingleberger. *Courtesy of Inglenook Winery.*

Niebaum Winery, August 15, 1896. In 1890, Niebaum hired F.A. Haber to begin an aggressive sales plan to introduce his wine into the marketplace. His wine was so well received that it was served at the White House to President Grover Cleveland. Haber did such a good job that Niebaum couldn't keep up with demand. He refused to bottle any more until it had been properly aged, so Haber reported that he couldn't fill any further orders for Inglenook. *Courtesy of Inglenook Winery.*

In 2011, Coppola finally secured the rights to the Inglenook name and the use of the chateau image. The Inglenook estate is now complete for the first time since 1964. During John Daniel's era, Inglenook built a reputation as the source of some of the finest wines ever made. Today, in addition to the Cabernet Sauvignon that dominates the estate, the Inglenook acreage is also planted with Zinfandel, Cabernet Franc, Merlot, Syrah and six acres of white Rhone varieties, which produce the estate's flagship white, Blancaneaux. Inglenook is now completely restored to its original dimensions.

Cedar Knoll Vineyard and Winery was founded in 1881 by Henry Hagen. Hagen produced wines that garnered many awards, including a silver medal at the Paris Exposition of 1889. During that era, Cedar Knoll was one of Napa's premier wineries. The vineyards survived the phylloxera infestation, but they could not survive prohibition. The winery fell into disrepair, and the vineyards lay fallow for nearly eighty years. Today, the vineyards are burgeoning, the restored Hagen house is a family home again and the winery has been reinvented. The Palmazes bought a forgotten stone winery, a fine old house badly in need of renovation and acres of land that had once produced fine Napa wines. Palmaz Vineyards makes a Cabernet Sauvignon under the old Cedar Knoll label.

In 1881, Villa Mt. Eden was founded as the eleventh bonded winery in Napa Valley by George W. Meyers of Oakland. He originally planted the land to Zinfandel and Riesling. In 1884, when winemaking began on-site, an estimated 6,500 gallons of wine were produced. In 1890, the winery had a 360-ton crush. In 1913, Nick Fagiani bought the winery, which he owned throughout prohibition.

According to Villa Mt. Eden, "It's unclear whether he sold grapes or continued to produce wine for medicinal or sacramental purposes. The winery changed hands a few times between the 1940s and 1960s, but the majority of that time it was owned by Constantine Ramsey, and grapes were sold to Beaulieu. In 1969 James and Anne McWilliams of San Francisco bought the winery, and expanded the number of varietals grown."

In January 1882, the San Francisco entrepreneur Alfred L. Tubbs owned 254 acres of rugged land just two miles north of Calistoga at the base of Mount Saint Helena. First Tubbs planted his vineyards, and then he built his chateau; in 1886, he imported a French-born winemaker. By 1896, his winery, christened Chateau Montelena (a contracted form of Mount Saint

Alfred Tubbs, Chateau Montelena. Tubbs was born in Deering, New Hampshire, in 1827 and sailed to California in 1849. Before opening Montelena, Tubbs had a rope factory in San Francisco and served in the legislature. He was married to Elizabeth, and they had four children. *Courtesy of Chateau Montelena Winery.*

Helena), was the seventh largest in the Napa Valley. On December 26, 1896, Tubbs passed away of heart failure at the Palace Hotel in San Francisco. At the time of his death, he was the president of the Tubbs Cordage Company, director of the Southern Pacific Railway and trustee of the Leland Stanford Jr. University. All that was in addition to his extensive vineyards. His wife, Elizabeth, along with her daughter, Nettie, and her son-in-law, Joseph Oyster, as well as her grandchildren, lived at the family home in San Francisco.

Montelena continued to operate until prohibition shut it down. The Tubbs family continued to harvest the vineyard and sold their grapes to other wineries for sacrament and home use. In 1934, after the repeal of prohibition, the winery and cellar were refurbished. Alfred's grandson, Chapin, was quoted in a newspaper interview saying, "It is my hope that the wine makers of this district will be able to prove to the world the excellence of our products, thereby bringing fame to this beautiful and fruitful country." He was right, and the Barrett family bought the property in 1972. Shortly thereafter, Chateau Montelena stunned the wine world with its win at the 1976 Paris Tasting. This Paris tasting was the basis for the movie *Bottle Shock*. Under the leadership of Jim Barrett, Chateau Montelena's Chardonnay was selected as the top-rated wine over four white Burgundies and six other California Chardonnays in Paris. Refusing to rest on their laurels, the Barrett family has continued their forward thinking, constantly seeking out ways to improve and perfect every aspect of the estate, from winemaking to grape growing to hospitality. Forty years ago, Chateau Montelena set out to define a style, and in 1972, Jim Barrett did just that with the winery's now famous Chardonnay.

Spottswoode Estate Vineyard & Winery traces its history back to the early 1880s and a man named George Schonewald. George was a young German immigrant who resided in Hot Springs Township (near Calistoga today) in Napa County in 1870, and he owned a restaurant there. He found his way to White Sulphur Springs in about 1874, and there George met and married a young Irish woman named Catherine Quinn. By 1876, he was managing the luxurious Lick House in San Francisco, but he was soon out of a job when Lick died and the hotel became embroiled in a lawsuit.

In 1882, George was managing the Hotel Del Monte in Monterrey and was also the postmaster. It's believed that it was around this time when he purchased the land to build his vacation home in St. Helena. In 1884, he sold to Frank Kraft some of his land adjacent to the spot where he and Catherine would build their vacation home. After Frank acquired the land from George, he built a grand farmhouse and a stone wine cellar. George left the Hotel Del Monte, and the *San Francisco Bulletin* announced that on March 1, 1886, George would "take charge" of the Palace Hotel in San Francisco. E.T.M. Simmons, who was his bookkeeper, replaced him at Del Monte. In April 1887, George was back at the Hotel Del Monte in Monterrey but would soon be out of a job. It turns out that Simmons was a convicted thief well into debt, and he was arrested for setting a massive blaze that destroyed the hotel.

Spottswoode Vineyard. Susan Russell Johnstone-Spotts was born in Iowa in September 1859. She was the daughter of Reverend Alexander Johnstone. She married Albert in 1890, and the couple lived in San Francisco in 1900. In 1909, Susan became the secretary of San Francisco's orphanage. In 1920, she cared for a foster child named Catherine Schmidt. *Courtesy of Spottswoode Estate Vineyard and Winery.*

In 1889, George and Catherine began construction of a vacation home in St. Helena they called Esmeralda. The house was designed after the Hotel Del Monte, with Canary Island date palms, oak and cedar trees and olive trees. By 1890, the Hotel Del Monte had been rebuilt, and George was once again in charge, staying there until 1894. By 1895, George had taken charge of the Castle Crag Tavern and resort in Shasta County, which operated from June to October. His former boss, Charles Crocker, who owned the Hotel Del Monte, had his summer resort there. He managed both businesses until 1900, when the tavern's building was struck by lightning and destroyed. In 1903, the *San Jose Mercury News* reported that Schonewald would be the new manager of the Hotel Del Coronado in San Diego. Almost one year later, San Diego's *Evening Tribune* reported that he was retiring due to continued ill health. He and Catherine then moved to their country home in St. Helena.

Upon Catherine's death in 1905, George sold Esmeralda to Joseph Bliss, who renamed the property Stonehurst. In 1908, Bliss sold the property to Dr. George Allen, who again changed the name, to Lyndenhurst. Just two years later, Allen and his wife sold the property to Mrs. Susan Spotts. She appropriately named the home Spottswoode in memory of her late husband, who passed away on Valentine's Day in 1909. Albert Tunstall Spotts was the coiner at the San Francisco Mint and was the nephew of Admiral Harry Spotts of Kentucky. He also served as city and county recorder in San Francisco and managed the California Title Insurance Company.

Despite prohibition nearing, Spotts and her farmworkers planted a field blend of Green Hungarian, French Colombard and Petite Sirah grapes. While the winery suffered under prohibition, they managed to sell their fruit to Christian Brothers Winery, which was making sacramental wine. Susan also earned extra income by growing mushrooms in the basement and raising frogs for the newest gourmet trend of frog legs. The property eventually passed to Mrs. Spotts's niece, Catherine Bielsky, and in 1972, the Novak family bought the winery. Today, Spottswoode uses Frank Kraft's cellars to house their sleeping wine.

Before settlers moved into the Napa Valley in the 1830s and 1840s, the area surrounding the V Madrone winery and vineyard was home to the Wappo tribe. In 1883, August and Frederika Hersch acquired the property and built a Victorian house and winery at the location of V Madrone. The Hersches produced up to twenty thousand gallons of wine yearly at the August Hersch Winery. Claret was produced, and large quantities were shipped to New York customers. In 1894, August Hersch passed away prematurely, and shortly thereafter, the winery and its cooperage were sold. Several owners later, the winery was lost to history in the years following prohibition. In the early twentieth century, the property was transformed into a popular lodge and restaurant that became widely known in the 1930s and 1940s as The Madrones, named after the then numerous twisted red bark Madrone trees located in the area. Following the Hersches' ownership, the property was owned by several families until Chris and Pauline Tilley acquired it in 2001. From the end of the Hersches' ownership in the 1890s until 2001, the eight-acre property was largely fallow. In 2002, three and one-quarter acres of estate Cabernet Sauvignon were planted. Combining the legacy of the nineteenth-century vineyard and the twentieth-century lodge, Chris and Pauline Tilley named the restored winery V Madrone.

Christian "Chris" Pugh Adamson was born in Germany and arrived in San Francisco in April 1854. He headed north, where he first worked for W.A. Fisher until 1856, when he went to the Yuba River area to pursue mining. During the following twelve years, he fought Indians, mined and farmed. By 1870, he had purchased 173 acres from George C. Yount's estate for about $10,000. In 1879, the *St. Helena Star* reported that Adamson had "now thirty acres of grapes and expects to put in many more, finding them the best crop he can raise." In 1878, the forty-four-year-old married nineteen-year-old Anna Elizabeth "Lizzie" Waldschmidt. By 1881, Adamson had 87 acres in vines and was selling his grapes to a local wine man named John Thomann. In late June 1884, forty-nine-year-old Adamson hired well-known winery builder Hamden W. McIntyre to complete his new wine cellar on his 175 acres in Rutherford.

Just as Adamson's wine business seemed to be on track for success, an odd personal tragedy hit him in 1883. As he prepared to head to Napa for a meeting, he found his wife lying bleeding on the floor in their house. A local woman named Mrs. Storey was known to provide abortion services and had apparently nicked one of Lizzie's ovaries, and she and the unborn child died. Even though Emma Storey was charged with murder for an abortion, the penal code read, "intent to procure a miscarriage," and she was set free. According to the Frog's Leap winery, "Oddly enough, when Chris remarried and his second wife gave birth to their first child, she was named Emma."

In September 1886, Adamson's cellar was 60 feet by 120 feet, and the *Star* reported that "at Chris Adamson's wine cellar, near Rutherford, recently [was] found…a scene of great activity." The following year, the paper noted that Adamson had one of the largest cellars in the Rutherford district and was known for his excellent wines. One of Adamson's wines won a medal at the 1889 World's Fair in Paris. That same year, the *Napa Register* noted that Adamson would make 120,000 gallons of wine from his own grapes, although he had a capacity of 250,000.

Adamson suffered yet another personal loss in 1893. According to Frog's Leap, "Adamson lost his second wife, Hannah, who 'accidentally in a fit of temporary insanity' swallowed a large portion of carbolic acid and died. It was also around this time when phylloxera had been eating its way through Napa Valley and other nearby areas. In 1896, Chris lost his property when the bank called the note for his loan of $66,000. He lived another twenty-one years before dying at the age of 83."

In 1994, John Williams brought his winery to the newly purchased Red Barn. He combined the names of Stag's Leap, where he started his winemaking career, and Frog Farm, where his early vintages were made, to create Frog's Leap.

Anton Nichelini was born in Switzerland in 1862, arrived in Sage Canyon in 1882 at the age of twenty and worked for Joshua Chauvet. Joshua not only mentored his own son, Henry, but also Anton, who quickly took on winemaking duties. Henry and Anton became friends, and in fact, Henry was responsible for introducing Anton to his future wife, Caterina Corda, also from the Ticino Canton of Switzerland. Henry eventually took over the Chauvet empire—this was not only useful to Anton in keeping up with

Anton Nichelini. Anton and Caterina were married in 1882, and they had several children. In addition to his grapes, Anton had a mine of magnasite, which is used to make gunpowder. *Courtesy of Nichelini Winery.*

winemaking technology and grape growing varieties and techniques but was also just good business sense. Anton Nichelini was granted winery bond no. 843 in 1884 when he began his winery. While traveling on horseback, homesteaders Anton and Caterina became the first Swiss settlers in Napa County's Chiles Valley. They quickly set about planting vines and olive trees, and by 1895, they had constructed a hand-hewn stone winery with a seven-bedroom house above it. This would provide a home for the Nichelinis and their eventual twelve children. The estate was composed of 160 acres, and Nichelini also had the prospects of two good mines on his land—one of copper and the other of chrome. It was reported that "[o]n account of the mineral deposits, this farm is one of the most valuable in the county."

Between 1916 and 1933, Anton's wine business grew, and he developed both new vineyards and expanded his household wine delivery service throughout the Oakland East Bay area. Zinfandel grapevines that he planted in 1928 are still in production today. His local wine delivery business continued to grow through 1945 despite his death in 1937. The Nichelini presence expanded into key restaurants and select wine stores in San Francisco. Even the governor's house wine was Nichelini. Over the next fifteen years, the Nichelinis further expanded the vineyards with new varietals to meet the rising demand for blended, sweeter wines with generic names like Sauterne, Vin Rosé and Chablis. Nichelini Sauvignon Vert grapevines planted in 1946, today called Muscadelle de Bordelais, are still in production. Today, the Nichelini Winery has 540 acres, and its vision is expressed on its wine label, which portrays its roots with an iconic image of the old stone cellar. The winery, original Roman wine press and house still stand today and have remained in the family's hands for more than 120 years.

The Frank Family Winery was first constructed as the Larkmead Winery in 1884, and the building was refinished with native sandstone from the nearby hills in 1906. The massive stone edifice still stands today; it is on the National Register of Historical Places and is listed as a Point of Historical Interest in the state of California. Owners Richard Frank and Connie Frank focus their energies on making superb still wines. The winery produces Chardonnay, Zinfandel, Sangiovese and several distinctly different Cabernet Sauvignons.

Far Niente was founded in 1885 by John Benson, who was a forty-niner of the California gold rush and uncle of the famous American impressionist painter Winslow Homer. Benson wasn't new to viticulture and had been growing grapes in Napa Valley since the mid-1860s. Pioneer Franklin Buck was a close friend who remembered Benson from 1852,

Chardonnay vines like these dot California's countryside. *Courtesy of Sherry Monahan.*

Far Niente, 1900. Pioneer Franklin Buck recalled of John Benson in 1881: "He took down the old house and built the new one at the same site and we have all the old farm buildings, two large barns, granary, carriage house, dairy house, etc. He has 500 acres of land nearly square, in the valley running back to the hills, and 300 acres of the hills…I am running a tunnel to increase the supply of water and shall set out about 3,000 grape vines." *Courtesy of Far Niente Winery.*

saying, "John Benson has become rich speculating and living easy and is, withal, a great ladies man."

Buck also recalled Benson from 1875 in this letter: "Received letters from Personnette, Cap Trufant and John Benson lately. They are all alive and scattered in different parts of the Pacific Slope. If you are fond of grapes you had better visit John's farm in Napa, California. He raised 600 tons last year and made 20,000 gallons of wine and quite a lot of raisins, but the enterprise doesn't pay." By 1881, Benson already had a ranch in Oakville and wanted his friend Franklin Buck to run it for him since he spent most of his time in San Francisco.

Benson hired architect Hamden W. McIntyre—creator of the former Christian Brothers Winery (now the Culinary Institute of America at

Greystone), Inglenook and Frog's Leap—to design his building. Constructed against a hillside in western Oakville, Far Niente functioned as a gravity-flow winery, gently moving the grapes through each stage of production. Far Niente prospered until the onset of prohibition in 1919, when it was abandoned and left to fall into disrepair. Sixty years later, in 1979, Gil and Beth Nickel purchased the winery and adjacent vineyard and began a three-year restoration of the property. During restoration, the original name, Far Niente, from an Italian phrase that romantically translates as "without a care," was found carved in stone on the front of the building, where it remains to this day. Far Niente's past and present were reunited in 1998 when a bottle of Far Niente Sweet Muscat, vintage 1886, was discovered in a private cellar in Marin County, California. The bottle exhibits the original label, cork and capsule. The label, featuring a sepia-tone line drawing of a hammock laden with grape clusters, is believed to have been designed by Benson's nephew, artist Winslow Homer. Historians of the artist liken the style of the hammock on the label to the same technique employed in Homer's other works.

The historic Bergfeld Winery was built in 1885 by a New England sea captain named William Peterson. After thirty-one years as a seaman and several circumnavigations around the globe, Captain Peterson set his sights on the Napa Valley and the pursuit of viticulture and winemaking. He moved to St. Helena and purchased forty-nine acres of land in 1873. He planted vineyards and soon began construction of his winery. Built of solid stone on the first floor and wood frame on the second, the five-thousand-square-foot winery had the capacity to produce twenty-seven thousand gallons of wine. Unfortunately, Captain Peterson did not enjoy the fruits of his labor for long, as phylloxera destroyed his vineyard in the early 1890s. Deeply discouraged, Captain Peterson sold his winery in 1894 and returned to his native Massachusetts, where he died six years later. The second owner was a San Francisco building contractor named Robert Bergfeld. He was a German immigrant who purchased the winery for a pittance and immediately set about replanting the vineyard. He also chiseled away Peterson's name from the stone above the winery entrance and replaced it with his own, "Bergfeld," which is how the winery remains today.

In 1906, the winery was purchased by Theodore Gier, who also owned what is now the Hess Collection winery. Gier was responsible for constructing the large barrel storage rooms that are adjacent to the historic winery. Gier held the winery until it was eventually shut down due to the onset of

Above: Hall Winery, Peterson building, circa 1890s. Originally planted in 1859 by New England sea captain William Peterson, the St. Helena Bergfeld vineyard was among the first in Napa Valley. The current owners named it Bergfeld in homage to wine pioneer Robert Bergfeld, who owned the property from 1894 to 1910. *Courtesy of Hall Wines.*

Left: William Peterson, circa 1890s. Peterson was born in about 1821 in Massachusetts and married an Englishwoman named Jane. *Courtesy of Hall Wines.*

prohibition. In 1933, with the repeal of prohibition, a small group of local vineyard owners led by Charles Forni and Angelo Petri formed the Napa Valley Cooperative Winery. The Halls acquired the historic winery in 2003, and Hall's Bergfeld Cabernet Sauvignon celebrates the legacy of pioneering wine grower Robert Bergfeld.

Italian winemaker Vittorio Sattui arrived in San Francisco in 1882 with his new bride, Kattarina, to begin their life in America. Born in Genoa, Vittorio, like his father before him, was by trade a baker from the small hill town of Carsi. In San Francisco, Vittorio at first worked as a baker, making wine in his spare time, while Kattarina took in washing. Soon, the industrious Sattui family had saved enough money to start a boardinghouse in the Italian colony of North Beach.

Vittorio continued to make wine, serving it to his patrons at the boardinghouse. By 1885, the reputation of Vittorio's wines allowed him to quit the bakery and devote himself full time to his real passion of winemaking. He quickly established a thriving commercial venture (located at 722 Montgomery, now Columbus Avenue) called St. Helena Wine Cellars, taking the name of the small, bucolic Napa Valley town where he obtained his grapes. Vittorio always said, "There is nothing like St. Helena grapes!" He would personally select the grapes during the harvest and then haul them by horse-drawn wagon to Napa for transfer to San Francisco by ferry.

When Vittorio moved his expanding winemaking business and family to the Mission district, he adopted the new name, V. Sattui Wine Company. Vittorio continued to ferry his grapes from St. Helena, crushing them at his new winery. The V. Sattui Wine Company's high-quality wines were sold directly to the customers and delivered to their houses in barrels and demijohns (usually one- to twenty-five-gallon sizes) throughout the Bay Area by horse-drawn wagon. Eventually, Vittorio's clients reached as far north as Oregon and Washington State, and the family business thrived. But in 1920, prohibition crippled Vittorio Sattui's family business. He said, "I'll do nothing against the law," and V. Sattui Wine Company lay dormant for the next sixty years.

Dario Sattui remembered visiting his great-grandfather, Vittorio, who continued to live upstairs at the long-dormant Bryant Street winery until his death at age ninety-four. He recalled, "As a small child, my first recollection was the aroma of wine emanating from the old building as soon as I entered." He played among the barrels and ovals in the cellars, stories of the old family wine business ringing in his ears. It was then, Dario believes, that the dream of reopening the winery began. But just how to do that was the problem. Dario had almost no capital and little practical knowledge of the wine industry. So, he dedicated himself to developing the tools and skills he'd need to make the dream become a reality.

By 1985, V. Sattui Winery was able to build a beautiful stone winery amid the venerable 250-year-old oaks, reminiscent of the late nineteenth-century wineries in Italy and France. With its two stories, tower, wine caves and underground aging cellars, its completion was a fitting tribute to help celebrate the centennial of Vittorio's dream. That same year, the thirty-four-acre vineyard adjacent to the winery became available. From the very beginning, Dario refused to compromise on the quality of the wine. The

---

TIRAMISU

8 egg yolks, room temperature
8 tbsp. granulated sugar
⅓ c. plus 2 tbsp. V. Sattui Madeira
2 8-oz. containers mascarpone cheese
1½ c. espresso coffee, freshly brewed, room temperature
38 ladyfingers
cocoa powder

Beat together eggs and sugar in electric mixer for approximately 4–5 minutes or until thick and creamy. Add 2 tbsp. Madeira and the 2 8-oz. containers of mascarpone cheese. Gently but thoroughly mix together. Set aside.

Mix together espresso and remaining Madeira.

Line a serving dish with half of the ladyfingers. Pour half of the coffee/Madeira mixture over the ladyfingers, going slowly so it soaks in and covers the surface. Gently smooth half the filling mixture over the ladyfingers. Dust with cocoa.

Make another layer with the remaining ladyfingers, dipping each one in the remaining coffee/Madeira mixture before placing it in the dish. Cover with the remaining filling. Dust with cocoa. Chill for at least one hour before serving.

Recipe courtesy of Chef Gerardo Sainato at V. Sattui Winery.

production and retailing concept offers insight into the reasons for V. Sattui Winery's success. V. Sattui recommends its Madeira to taste their history in a bottle: "It's solera-made, wood-aged wine, and fortified with brandy. Our Solera is over 120 years old, and is one of the oldest in the U.S. The solera process is an ingenious system of fractional blending perfected by the Spanish to ensure consistent quality, based on the fact that old wines can be refreshed by the addition of a younger wine, which then acquires the characteristics of the old wine. We begin with now what is now a 107-year-old vintage port, a lasting vestige from Vittorio Sattui's original winery, as the 'mother,' or master-blend." Imagine a sourdough starter for wine.

The Varozza winery can trace its St. Helena roots back to 1885 as well. Emil Zange was born in Saxony, Germany, in 1834, arrived in America in about 1852 and can be traced back to Marysville, California, from 1857, when he became a citizen. In 1866, while in Marysville, he worked as a clerk. Next, he went to San Francisco in 1868 and became a furrier with Adolph Muller. From 1869 to 1874, he had his own grocery and liquor store, called Emil Zange and Company. During this time in 1870, Emil married Anna "Mary" Seiss, who had come to America in about 1860. The childless couple moved to St. Helena about ten years later, and he became a vine grower. Feeling ready to settle, Emil hired local artisans to build his two-story stone and wood winery built in 1885. He produced thirty-six thousand gallons of wine that year and in 1886 produced thirty-five thousand. In 1912, all appeared to be going well, until his wife, Mary, died at the age of sixty-eight. He sold his winery that same year. Emil only lived three years after his wife, and they are buried together in St. Helena.

Enter St. Helena resident Joseph Varozza, who bought Emil's business in 1913. Joseph worked in the vineyard at the top of Spring Mountain and also worked at the Bale Gristmill as a foreman. He and his wife, Jennie, had three children: Joseph, Meile and Elva. They returned to Switzerland for five years when Joseph was two but returned to St. Helena five years later. Joseph grew up on Spring Street; he worked at and then purchased the local blacksmith shop. He owned six hundred acres on what is now Langtree Road. He married his first wife, Mary, and they had three children: Robert, June and James. After an injury that required him to sell the blacksmith shop, Joseph purchased the property on Pratt Avenue (then called Hudson Avenue).

Joseph married his second wife, Mary Rossini (her father, Carlo, had vineyards and made wine in what is now Bell Canyon), and they raised four children at the ranch: Charlie, Josie, Alice and Harold. Joseph continued to produce wine here until he passed away in 1946. Harold was in the service during World War II and never really had a chance to make wine with his father. Mary sold the last of the wines, and they began selling the grapes to the other wineries. Harold purchased the ranch from his mother and continued to take care of the vineyards and sell the grapes. He and his wife, Irene, built a home on the property, and Jack was born and raised here. Jack worked in the vineyard with his dad, and in 1986, he moved into the home that his grandfather purchased from Zange.

While the Ehlers estate vine growing history begins in 1886, its history goes back much farther. It begins with an English physician named Edward Turner Bale, who had married General Vallejo's niece and was awarded a seventeen-thousand-acre land grant in 1841. Bale had hired metalworker Florentine Kellogg to construct the now historic Bale Gristmill. Kellogg, who was paid in land by Bale, soon left to pan for gold in the Sierra Nevadas. Possibly to fund his venture, he sold a portion of his land to newcomer Reverend Theodore Lyman, who was from Trinity Episcopal Church in San Francisco. Lyman, who saw the potential for wine production, was suddenly called to be bishop of North Carolina, and he gave the land to his son, W.W. Lyman.

W.W. Lyman was also a religious man and helped found Grace Episcopal Church of St. Helena. In 1882, W.W. Lyman sold the estate land to Reverend Alfred Todhunter. Although Todhunter planted ten acres of vines, the root louse phylloxera was already making its presence known in the Napa Valley. In 1885, faced with a dying vineyard, Todhunter sold his property to Sacramento grocer Bernard Ehlers for $7,000 in gold coin.

In 1886, Bernard Ehlers completed planting the vineyards and constructed the stone winery building, which remains. When Ehlers passed away in 1901, he left the estate to his wife, Anna, who maintained the property for the next fifteen years. During prohibition, local resident Alfred Domingos purchased the land from Anna Ehlers in 1923. Since home winemaking was legal, Domingos and his brother bootlegged wine and brandy to a growing stream of Bay Area visitors. In fact, so many tourists came to Napa Valley to obtain illegal alcohol that the Carquinez Bridge was erected to facilitate transportation. When prohibition ended, the Domingos brothers established the Old Bale Mill Winery, which they ran successfully until 1958.

In 1982, Parisians Jean and Sylviane Leducq established the Prince Michel Vineyards and Winery in Virginia. Their goal was to marry their Gallic passion for fine wine and food with American history. Under the direction of French enologist Jacques Boissenot, the Leducqs purchased seven acres of vineyard in 1987 that were part of the original land tract belonging to W.W. Lyman. This land was replanted to the traditional Bordeaux varietals of Cabernet Sauvignon, Cabernet Franc, Merlot and Petit Verdot. The Leducqs continued to acquire contiguous parcels as they came on the market. In May 2001, the original stone winery and estate home built by Bernard Ehlers was purchased, thus reuniting the estate.

Freemark Abbey began its history in 1886 when Josephine Marlin-Tychson established her redwood winery along Route 29 in St. Helena. She was one of eight children born to John and Eliza Marlin, who moved to Astoria, Oregon, in the mid-1800s. Josephine entered the world on March 25, 1855, in San Lorenzo, where she was raised. Her mother, Eliza, died when she was eight, and her father, John, married Eliza's sister, but it appears the marriage was more of an arrangement to raise eight children than one of love.

Josephine ended up marrying her brother-in-law after her sister Kate died in 1874—just three months after being married. About two years later, Josephine married Danish immigrant John Tychson on January 14, 1877. A year later, the two were the proud parents of daughter Annette. They left for Denmark in 1879 so John could settle some family affairs, and when they returned, they purchased twenty-six acres of vineyards and other holdings in St. Helena from former sea captain William James Sayward in 1881. Sayward had acquired the land from Charles Krug and called it the Lodi Ranch. As the happy couple worked to expand the vineyards and winery, John suffered from tuberculosis. In the spring, Josephine traveled to San Lorenzo to visit family, and while there, she became sick. While she was in bed, she received the tragic news that her husband and partner drove to Oakland, rented a room and proceeded to commit suicide. Josephine now faced the task of running the business alone and raising two small children.

She remained committed to seeing their dream through and forged ahead. Under her supervision, a fifty- by fifty-foot redwood structure was erected just in time for her first crush in 1886. She also built a cellar with a capacity of between twenty thousand and thirty thousand gallons of wine. In 1891, Josephine had fifty-five acres of grape bearing vines, which included Zinfandel, Riesling and Burgundy. In 1893, phylloxera was attacking Napa Valley, and Josephine lost ten acres to it. It's possible she sold the winery to her foreman, Nels Larson, in 1894 because of it. She never remarried and bought a white house across the street for her winery.

Josephine Tychson, circa 1880s. Josephine would kick off a history of innovation and become the first woman to build a commercially producing winery. *Courtesy of Freemark Abbey.*

Nels eventually sold the winery to Josephine's friend, Anton Forni, in 1898. He renamed the winery Lombarda Cellars, after his birthplace in Italy. In 1899, he constructed the stone winery, made of hand-strewn stones from nearby Glass Mountain, and it is still used for barrel storage. Forni ran the winery until his death in 1912, but his family kept the business going until prohibition.

The winery remained closed for twenty years during that time, until three businessmen from Southern California—Charles Freeman, Marquand Foster and Albert "Abbey" Ahem—purchased Lombarda Cellars and combined their names to reopen the winery as Freemark Abbey in 1939. Seven partners purchased the winery in 1968. Owners Dick Heggie, Brad Webb, Bill Jaeger, Frank Laurie Wood, Jim Warren, Chuck Carpy and John Bryan introduced Freemark Abbey's signature style of Chardonnay and Cabernet Sauvignon, and the winery earned the name University of Freemark. In 1976, Freemark Abbey was one of twelve American wineries selected to participate in the historic Judgment of Paris tasting. Freemark Abbey still uses Zinfandel and Riesling grapes, like Josephine did, to make some of its wines.

At about the same time as Josephine was beginning her winery, Scottish sea captain Hamden McIntyre built Eshcol Winery for the Bank of Napa founders, brothers James and George Goodman. The history of this winery goes back even farther because the vines were planted as early as 1881 by then property owner David Emerson, who had forty acres. In late 1882, Emerson transferred his Emerson Ranch to the Goodman brothers, and by 1885, they had renamed it Eshcol Ranch. In 1886, McIntyre designed Eshcol Winery as a gravity-flow system, which was a horse-drawn winch that brought grapes to the third floor of the three-story structure for crushing. It allowed gravity to carry the grape juice to the second floor for fermenting; eventually, the wine descended to the first floor for aging. Eshcol was among a number of wineries that McIntyre designed during this period, including Frog's Leap, Far Niente and Inglenook.

By 1887, it had produced sixty-five thousand gallons of wine it its first estate crush of the season. In March 1888, at the Sixth Annual California State Viticultural Convention in San Francisco, it won first place for an 1886 Cabernet Sauvignon. Later that July, James died, but his brother, George, continued to run the winery. In 1889, Eshcol Winery won over half the awards at the France Exposition in 1889. In the late 1890s, phylloxera nearly brought wine production in Napa to an end, but men like Goodman replanted their vines. In 1895, Eshcol was leased to J. Clark Fawver, who was the son of Yountville wine pioneer Thomas Fawver. In 1904, George Goodman sold the winery to Fawver. George died in 1917 in Napa. The Eshcol Winery survived prohibition by making sacramental wines, and in 1933, it had its first crush and made a Claret. In 1941, J. Clark Fawver died, and the winery was leased to the Beringer brothers to store their wine.

By the time the Trefethen family purchased the property in 1968, the winery had fallen into serious disrepair. John and Janet committed themselves to restoring the building to its former glory. They carefully researched the winery's past and worked for years to restore it. Aside from replacing the dirt floor on the first level with concrete, they made no significant structural changes. The Trefethens' restoration efforts were recognized in 1988 by the Department of the Interior, which placed the winery on the National Register of Historic Places as the only nineteenth-century wooden gravity-flow winery

Eschol Winery, circa late 1800s. In the 1880s, the Goodman brothers had 280 acres, and 150 were devoted to vines that at the time were from one to three years old. They included Zinfandel, Lenoir, Matero, Chasselas, Riesling and Malbec, as well as the Riparia and California vines that were used to graft on. *Courtesy of Trefethen Family Vineyards.*

Eschol Winery, circa late 1800s. It's now known as Trefethen. *Courtesy of Trefethen Family Vineyards.*

surviving in Napa County. Trefethen still makes an award-winning Cabernet Sauvignon, just like the one Eshcol did (for which it won its 1886 award).

BAKED ZUCCHINI WITH MUSHROOM

4 zucchini
kosher salt
2 tbsp. olive oil
2 tbsp. butter
6 c. mushrooms, chopped, domestic or wild
1 clove garlic, finely chopped
2 tbsp. shallots, finely chopped
¼ c. Trefethen Chardonnay
2 tbsp. fresh tarragon, chopped
2 tbsp. fresh parsley, chopped
¼ c. Parmesan cheese, grated*
black pepper

Cut the four zucchini lengthwise into 8 halves. With a tablespoon, lightly core the halves to form a "boat" for the mushroom mixture. Place the zucchini on a baking sheet and sprinkle the halves with kosher salt.

In a saucepan on medium-high, heat the olive oil and butter. Add the mushrooms and sprinkle with a pinch of salt, stir and cover. Sauté the mushrooms until all their liquid has evaporated. Add the garlic and shallots and sauté 2–3 minutes. Add the Chardonnay and reduce the liquid, deglazing the pan. Add the tarragon and parsley and sauté for 1 minute. Remove from heat and stir in the Parmesan cheese. Salt and pepper to taste.

Spoon the mushroom mixture into the zucchini boats, place the halves in a 350-degree oven for 15–20 minutes until zucchini is medium-soft. *Note: you can omit Parmesan and top zucchini boats with plain goat cheese.

It is perfect with a chilled glass of Trefethen Estate Chardonnay on a warm summer afternoon!

Recipe courtesy of Trefethen Family Vineyards.

GRILLED TRI-TIP OF BEEF WITH
TREFETHEN CABERNET THYME SAUCE

2–3 lbs. tri-tip roast, trimmed
½ c. Trefethen Cabernet Sauvignon
1 tbsp. Worcestershire Sauce
2 cloves fresh garlic, minced
2 tsp. cracked black pepper
4 tbsp. extra virgin olive oil

Marinate the tri-tip with all of the ingredients for four hours or overnight. Grill on the barbecue or roast in the oven at 375 degrees until internal temperature reaches 130 degrees (medium-rare). While the meat is cooking, remove one slightly chilled 750ml bottle of Trefethen Vineyards S.I.N. from the refrigerator. Pour equal parts into wine glasses, enough to serve those in attendance and relax. The meat will take a little while to cook!

When the meat is up to temperature, remove from barbecue or oven and let rest for 15 minutes.

CABERNET THYME SAUCE

1 shallot, minced
2 tbsp. salted butter
½ c. Trefethen Vineyards Cabernet Sauvignon
½ c. beef or veal stock
1½ tsp. chopped fresh thyme
salt and pepper to taste

Sauté the shallot in the butter until soft. Add the Cabernet Sauvignon and stock and bring to a simmer, skimming off the top. Continue cooking over a low heat for 30 minutes. Strain through a fine strainer and add the chopped thyme. Season with salt and pepper to taste.

TO SERVE

Slice the meat against the grain and fan the slices out onto a warm platter. Pour the Cabernet thyme sauce over the meat. Serve with grilled summer vegetables and sweet corn, as well as, of course, a glass of Trefethen Vineyards Estate Cabernet Sauvignon!

Recipe courtesy of Trefethen Family Vineyards.

S.E. Chase Cellars pays homage to Sarah Esther Chase Bourn, a woman who, like the wine that bears her name, demonstrated incredible strength of character, an indelible personality and a take-notice presence.

Sarah was the wife a wealthy businessman who discovered the Napa Valley while visiting the area's spas in the late 1800s. But it was a tragedy that compelled her to create a home in the valley. After the loss of a young son, Sarah persuaded her husband, William Bourn, to purchase the Madrona estate, as it was known, on the southwestern edge of St. Helena. With a strong will and determination, Sarah turned the property into a working ranch. In addition to the vineyard that already existed, Sarah added chickens, olive trees, wheat, corn and even a silkworm farm to her holdings.

A colorful figure in the community, Sarah was noted as much for her travels to Europe with her daughters as her goings-on at Madrona. Her legacy became the vineyard that first attracted her to the property. Upon the death of her husband, the management of the estate was turned over to her son, William Bourn II, who was as industrious as his mother. William perpetuated Sarah's impact on the area by selling the family grapes to Charles Krug. It was the start of what would become a longstanding family tradition.

Not content to only sell grapes, William wanted to produce wine and create a place to do so for himself and his neighbors. The answer was to build a co-op for wine production and storage. In 1888, he built Greystone Cellars, the historic and formidable stone building at the northern end of St. Helena. In 1894, when phylloxera wiped out much of Napa Valley's vineyards, including Sarah's, William sold Greystone to the Christian brothers.

Less than ten years after the vineyard went fallow, William's sister, Maude, and her husband, William Alston Hayne, planted the eponymously named vineyard with Zinfandel and other varietals. Today, the Zinfandel vines still thrive. The head-pruned Zinfandel vines are dry-farmed in the sandy, gravelly soil that produces Napa Valley's most exuberant and robust Zinfandel grapes.

In 1998, Sarah's great-great-grandson, Andy Simpson, and his wife, Pam Simpson, harvested grapes from a twelve-acre parcel within the Hayne Vineyard and created their first vintage of S.E. Chase Family Cellars Zinfandel. Their Zinfandel vibrantly expresses the rich history of the Hayne Vineyard and the passion of the Chase family.

Pope Valley Winery is situated in Pope Valley, which was originally named for the Wappo Indians who lived there. The first white settler in Pope Valley was Julian Pope, from whom the valley derived its name. Ed Haus was born in Switzerland but left to find a new life in California. In 1882, he purchased a farm in Pope Valley and opened a blacksmith shop. Once Ed was able to get settled and put aside some money, he wrote back to his family to send out his childhood sweetheart, Ida Leimbacher, to become his wife. Swiss tradition allowed only the eldest girl to marry first, so to his surprise, the family sent out Ida's eldest sister, Bertha. Ed was disappointed but married Bertha, and they started a life together and had two children named Sam and Lillian.

Ed and Bertha founded the Burgundy Winery. The winery was constructed in 1897 from massive timbers moved down from the Oat Hill Quicksilver Mine. The winery is a three-story gravity-flow winery, with a hand-dug cave that took more than nine years to dig. During prohibition, the winery continued to do well. Ed's son, Sam, befriended a young man from Chicago while in the military. Through his connections, the Haus family began to take wine on a horse cart down to Napa, where it boarded a train and went to Chicago to be served in Al Capone's speakeasies and brothels. Eventually, Sam prudently stopped selling wine to the mob. To outside sources, it appeared that the winery ceased operations during prohibition and was reopened after its repeal.

Ed's children, Sam and Lily Haus, operated the winery until 1959, and in 1972, they sold it to the Devitt family. They, in turn, sold it in the mid-1990s. Longtime Pope Valley residents Jim, Sam and Henry Eakle; Ralf Gerdes; Manny Gomes; and Rodney Young joined together to purchase this historical winery in 1997. In 2009, the next generation of Eakles stepped in to continue building and furthering the family's vision for Pope Valley Winery as a fine winemaking establishment. Currently, siblings David Eakle as winemaker and Diana Eakle Hawkins as general manager are making great strides in brining Pope Valley Winery to the next level.

Rancho La Jota was founded in 1844 when Alta California was still under Mexican rule. Napa Valley pioneer George C. Yount asked Mexican general Mariano Vallejo for land on heavily forested Howell Mountain to provide lumber for settlers in the valley. Yount received 4,454 acres and named this spectacular land Rancho La Jota, which literally means "the letter J," possibly referring to a popular Spanish dance of the eighteenth and nineteenth centuries.

La Jota Vineyard Company was founded in the 1890s by Frederick Hess, who was an immigrant from Locarno, Switzerland, and who established a

Above: Vineyards, Far Niente. Vineyards like these have been dotting California's countryside since the 1800s. *Courtesy of Sherry Monahan.*

Left: A 1937 Burgundy wine, Foppiano. In 1937, the trailblazing Foppiano Wine Company began bottling wine under the Foppiano name—one of the first Sonoma County wineries to do so. *Courtesy of Sherry Monahan.*

Above: Seghesio old cellars. In 1903, Seghesio wines were being shipped via the railroad and sold in San Francisco from horse-drawn carts. *Courtesy of Sherry Monahan.*

Left: Schramsberg wine cellar. Robert Louis Stevens wrote, "I tasted every variety and shade of Schramberger, red and white Schramberger, Burgundy Schramberger, Schramberger Hock, Schramberger Golden Chasselas, the latter with a notable bouquet, and I fear to think how many more. Much of it goes to London—most, I think; and Mr. Schram has a great notion of the English taste." *Courtesy of Sherry Monahan.*

Inglenook vineyards. While the Niebaums never had any of their own children, Susie's niece and nephew moved in with them in 1887 when her brother, Francis, passed away in 1887. In 1900, Leah Shingleberger was nineteen, and her brother, Gustave Niebaum, was seventeen and attending school. *Courtesy of Sherry Monahan.*

Hall-Bergfeld vineyards. Robert Bergfeld was born in Hanover, Germany, and came to America in 1870. He married Elizabeth "Lizzie," and they had five children. Bergfeld only kept the winery for twelve years. *Courtesy of Hall Wines.*

Left: Langtry Old Vine. This old vine was planted by Lillie in 1885, and while it doesn't produce much wine, it's a testament to Lillie's dedication to grape growing. *Courtesy of Sherry Monahan.*

Below: Redmon winery. The winery sits on what was two large parcels fronting on Main Street (Highway 29), running east–west for a distance of 2,119 feet parallel to today's Dowdell Lane. They were of equal size, each measuring 28.63 acres. Together, the parcels reached a total of 57.26 acres. *Courtesy of Redmon.*

Left: Schramsberg sparkling wine. The caves maintain a consistent cool temperature, providing an environment that is paramount in the flavor development of bottled-aged sparkling wines. At any given time, as many as 2.7 million bottles are in the Schramsberg caves, aging two to ten years before release. *Courtesy of Sherry Monahan.*

Below: Redwood barrel. Most wineries in the 1800s used redwood to age their wines because it grew in the area. They later learned that it gave the wine a musty taste and smell. *Courtesy of Sherry Monahan.*

Above: Oak barrels. Oak barrels like these replaced the redwood ones. Some oak was from the U.S. while others were imported in from France. *Courtesy of Sherry Monahan.*

Left: Kunde old vine. Several of these beautiful old vines grow in the Kunde vineyards. They are much more fragile than they look. *Courtesy of Sherry Monahan.*

Above: Italian Swiss Colony winery. In 1892, it sold Claret from between forty-five and sixty-five cents per bottle. *Courtesy of Sherry Monahan.*

Left: Nichelini residence. Anton Nichelini and his family lived in this cabin when they first settled on the land. The family keeps it up in their memory. *Courtesy of Sherry Monahan.*

Schramsberg winery. Once called Schramsberger wine, it continually received high accolades. The Lewis Publishing Company in 1891 wrote that "the hillsides for grape-culture, have all been put into profitable use by Mr. and Mrs. Schram; and hence it is they who chose the admirable location in the foot-hills and are now reaping the return for the greater labor of clearing those hillsides, in the superior quality of the Schramsberger Riesling, Hock and Burgundy, that have become so celebrated." *Courtesy of Sherry Monahan.*

Sebantiani press. This press is part of the original collection that Samuele Sebantiani used when he took over the winery. It dates to the late 1800s to early 1900s. *Courtesy of Sherry Monahan.*

Left: Chardonnay vines. These vines are just beginning to blossom and show signs of fruit in late April. *Courtesy of Sherry Monahan.*

Below: Buena Vista Brut. Agoston Haraszthy's son, Arpad, spent more than two years in France learning the craft of sparkling wine and used Méthode Traditionelle to make sparkling wine. Arpad's sparkling wine, Eclipse, was one of the most celebrated in the nineteenth century; this is Buena Vista's tribute to him. *Courtesy of Sherry Monahan.*

Bucklin Fields. This is the old Hill Ranch planted by William McPherson Hill in 1851. He experimented with a variety of vines, which resulted in a mixed-field blend of grapes. The December 1871 *Pacific Rural Press* reported, "We sampled a bottle of wine from the cellar of Wm. McPherson Hill made from the Zinfandel grape, a new variety that is growing in favor with winemakers. The wine was pronounced by the gentlemen who tasted it to be superior to any they had seen in the state." *Courtesy of Sherry Monahan.*

Buena Vista Winery. This is the original winery building built by Agoston Haraszthy in the 1850s and serves as the tasting room today. *Courtesy of Sherry Monahan.*

Left: "The Count." Sonoma actor George Webber portrays Agoston Haraszthy at Buena Vista's Winery. *Courtesy of Sherry Monahan.*

Below: Healdsburg chickens. Even chickens like to wander around the vineyards and surrounding flower beds in California's wine country. *Courtesy of Larry Monahan.*

Left: Old Inglenook bottles. These historic wine bottles from the 1870s are stored in private tasting rooms at Inglenook. *Courtesy of Sherry Monahan.*

Below: Chiles House. Colonel Joseph Ballinger Chiles was another early settler who was granted land from General Vallejo. His grant is in modern-day Chiles Valley. In 1854, Colonel Chiles brought his wife, Margaret, to California and settled on one thousand acres, now the site of Rutherford. He built this house in 1856 and resided in it for many years. This home, now on the Inglenook estate, is one of the oldest houses in Napa Valley. *Courtesy of Sherry Monahan.*

Above: Italian-Swiss Wine Colony. This house, called the Villa Pompeii, was built in 1902 for the express purpose of hosting guests to visit, taste, tour and experience the wines and associated lifestyle of the Italian Swiss Agricultural Colony at Asti. *Courtesy of Sherry Monahan.*

Left: Langtry Estates. The rock remains of Lillie Langtry's wine estate. *Courtesy of Sherry Monahan.*

Left: Nichelini Winery. The winery has a beautiful picnic area behind the historic Nichelini home and tasting room. Bring your lunch and enjoy the serenity of the tree-draped hideaway. *Courtesy of Sherry Monahan.*

Below: Schramsberg housing. This building was erected to house the Chinese immigrants who worked at the winery digging the caves. *Courtesy of Sherry Monahan.*

Above: Schramsberg home. As they continued to prosper, the Schrams built this lavish Victorian home that replaced the original cabin. A shipbuilder and his team were hired for the construction, and small pegs were used in place of more modern nails. The house became a gathering spot for the many friends and colleagues with whom the Schrams had become familiar. The Schram house is still lived in to this day and retains its spirit of hospitality. *Courtesy of Sherry Monahan.*

Left: Sebastiani Vineyards and Winery tasting room. Sample Sebastiani wines in their historic 1870s building in Sonoma, California. This building is where they used to make the wine. *Courtesy of Sherry Monahan.*

Sebastiani Vineyards and Winery tank. This is one of the original 1904 tanks used to hold Samuele Sebastiani's wine. *Courtesy of Sherry Monahan.*

Sebastiani Vineyards and Winery barrel. This is one of the original redwood barrels that Samuele Sebastiani used to age his wine. *Courtesy of Sherry Monahan.*

German-language newspaper in San Francisco. No doubt influenced by other European immigrants involved in California's wine industry, Hess purchased 327 acres of Rancho La Jota, high on Howell Mountain, for his vineyards. In 1898, he built the winery from volcanic ash rock quarried right on the property. The wines of La Jota, only two years after the winery's construction, won a bronze medal at the 1900 Paris Exposition. In 1904, they won gold at the World's Fair in St. Louis. Today, the winery's flagship wine is its Cabernet Sauvignon.

In 1900, when Georges de Latour's wife, Fernande, first laid eyes on the land that would become their original Rutherford vineyard, she named it "beau lieu," or "beautiful place." Shortly thereafter, De Latour sold his thriving cream of tartar business, bought the four-acre ranch and founded Beaulieu Vineyard with the vision of making Napa Valley wines that would rival those of his native France. De Latour quickly made a name for himself by importing phylloxera-resistant rootstock from Europe to the recently ravaged fledgling California wine industry.

Beaulieu Vineyard began selling sacramental wine to the Catholic Church, establishing a strong relationship that would allow Beaulieu Vineyard to become the only Napa Valley winery to remain in business during prohibition. Not only did it remain, but it also increased its business fourfold. After the repeal in 1933, De Latour began searching for someone who could contribute European winemaking expertise. In 1938, he traveled to France and returned with André Tchelistcheff. He tasted the De Latour family's private wine, which they called Private Reserve, from the 1936 vintage. This Cabernet Sauvignon–based wine was so distinctive that Tchelistcheff insisted it be bottled and sold as the winery's flagship offering. The result was the inaugural release of Georges de Latour Private Reserve Cabernet Sauvignon.

The Redmon Winery can trace its wine roots back to 1898, but the land could have been planted to grapes before then. According to Lisa Redmon-Mangelson:

> *The parcel on which the house sits has been traced back being part of a larger landholding on which at least one winery operated. It was once owned by Dr. Beldon Crane's estate and later willed to Edward and Abe McPike in October 1898. On December 3, 1907, William Frederick Bornhorst and Mrs. William (Elizabeth Warns) Ebeling purchased the property from*

G.W. Teale and his wife, Kate L. Teale. Mrs. Ebeling was the wife of Mr. Bornhorst's then business partner, William Ebeling. Mr. Ebeling died in St. Helena on March 9, 1910. The widow Ebeling married William Bornhorst the next year. Bornhorst and Ebeling had entered into partnership in 1892 to produce wine in Calistoga, and they built a wine cellar there and planted forty acres of vineyard, according to the account by Tom Gregory in his History of Solano and Napa Counties California.

That winery was known as Bornhorst and Ebeling. Just before the death of William Bornhorst in 1922, the couple sold the property, including both of the original 28.63-acre lots that once belonged to Dr. Crane. In just over a month, the property had changed hands again, and in the fall of the following year, it was sold yet again to Louis E. Engelberg, who took title to the property on September 29, 1923. However, the sellers, Vittorio Lavagnino and his wife, Caterina—together with a man named C. Garibotti and his wife—reserved possession of the premises until November 15 of that year for "the purpose of harvesting 1923 crop of grapes now growing on said premises, according to the deed."

Chapter 3

SONOMA PIONEERS

Although Sonoma began as a mission and had mission grapes, it only took until the mid-1850s for them to be recognized for their nonmission wine. A headline in the *Daily Alta* on December 6, 1858, read, "Wine Culture in Sonoma." The story noted, "The wine of Sonoma is different from that of the Southern portion of the State, being lighter and more like French wines."

Hubert Bancroft noted that the early popular grapes in the 1850s were Zinfandel and Riesling, brought over from Europe. By the end of the 1880s, grape varietals included Alexandrian Muscat, Zinfandel, Riesling, White St. Peter, Madeline Blanche, Black July, Sweetwater, Shasselas and Fontainebleau. Fall grapes included Muscatel, White Malaga, Rose of Peru, Red Tokay, Cornichon, Berger, Malvoisie, Charbonneau and seedless Sultana. One of the first known persons to plant nonmission grapes in Sonoma was William McPherson Hill (see *Historic Vineyards*).

Colonel Agoston Haraszthy de Mokesa was born into Hungarian royalty in 1812 but set his sights on the New World. He arrived in America in 1840 and settled in Wisconsin, where he was the first to plant hops to make beer. His grape growing efforts there failed due to the cold climate, so he traveled to California in 1849. Surprisingly, he headed for San Diego, despite there being gold fever up north. Although he became the first lawman in San Diego and rose to the assembly, his grape growing efforts failed once again. Determined to find the perfect place to plant his vines, the self-proclaimed "Count" headed north.

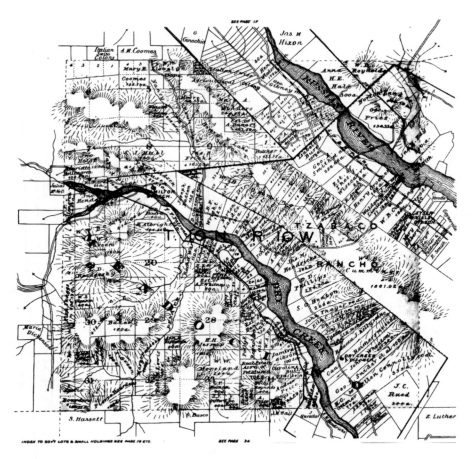

Sonoma map, 1898. Sonoma County has become one of the best grape growing areas in California. *Courtesy of Library of Congress.*

In 1852, he purchased 120 acres just south of San Francisco near the Mission Dolores. This time, the dense fog crippled his vineyard attempts, so he placed his dreams of "purple gold" on hold. He earned a living as an assayer for those lucky enough to find gold. Then, in 1856, he purchased the 800-acre Buena Vista ranch in Sonoma. It was around this time when he received an important shipment from his native Hungary that included six choice rooted vines and 160 cuttings. Also in the package were two small bundles—one was the Muscat of Alexandria, and the other was said to be Zinfandel. In 1857, the Count excavated Sonoma's first caves for storing and aging wine. That same year, his vineyards produced 6,500 gallons in the

The Count, circa 1860s. According to author Vincent Carosso, "This colorful Hungarian is responsible for propagating the choice varieties of European viniferas in California...The limited use Vignes made of European vines was experimental, Haraszthy laid the basis for the making of Zinfandel, the Malvoisie, and many other varieties commercially and viniculturally important."
Courtesy of Buena Vista Winery.

first vintage, and by 1860, more than 250 acres of wines had been planted. Others followed, including a friend he made in San Francisco by the name of Charles Krug. Krug purchased land from his friend the Count but later moved to Napa, where he borrowed one of the Count's presses to crush his first grapes.

The Count used Buena Vista to experiment with a variety of things related to viticulture. He created the first gravity-flow winery, which allows the grapes to gently fall into the tanks without bruising them. Quite the innovator, he's also credited with championing non-irrigation. Until he proved that the vines planted without it actually survived, the planting areas in Northern California were limited. He's also credited with experimenting with redwood barrels to age wine.

Buena Vista bottling line, 1865. Haraszthy arrived in Sonoma, which had already made history following the Bear Flag Revolt. With his first glimpse of Sonoma Valley and its rich soil, the Count sensed instantly that his search for a perfect grape growing region had ended. *Courtesy of Buena Vista Winery.*

In 1861, he persuaded the state to let him make a tour of European wine growing countries to study and report on the methods being used. He and his son, Arpad, returned in 1862, carrying more than three hundred different varietals. By doing this, Haraszthy inspired winemakers in California to experiment with many varieties of grapes. The Count and others, including Charles Wetmore, planted mixed field blends with several varieties in one vineyard just to see which ones worked and which one didn't.

The Buena Vista Vinicultural Society (BVVS) was established in 1863 by Haraszthy to improve the winery's winemaking prowess. (Note this was called "vinicultural," which is the business of growing grapes and making wine, and not "viticultural.") When the Count formed the BVVS, he needed investors, and some were prominent San Francisco investment bankers. Even though Haraszthy had grand plans and knew that the California wine

Buena Vista barrel washing, circa late 1800s. In 1857, on what was already known as Buena Vista Ranch, the Count constructed an elaborate home and a beautiful stone winery and planted his first Sonoma vineyards. The first vintage produced 6,500 gallons. Buena Vista continued to grow and expand, and by 1860, more than 250 acres of vines had been planted. *Courtesy of Buena Vista Winery.*

industry would flourish one day, he was ahead of his time. Despite having a successful first year, the Count's ambitions exceeded the demand for California, and his investors forced him out of the society.

Crushed, he left Buena Vista and headed for Nicaragua to look into the sugar and rum trade. In 1869, Haraszthy was crossing an alligator-infested stream when he fell from a tree branch. The flamboyant Count was never seen or heard from again. Despite winning accolades for its wine in 1873 in London, Vienna, Australia, Chile, Japan and Paris, the Buena Vista Winery succumbed to financial pressures, and in 1878, the estate was auctioned off. His son, Arpad, continued to make wine and created the Eclipse champagne in the 1880s by using grapes from the Orleans Vineyards. His father's Buena Vista Winery laid dormant into the 1940s. In 2011, the Boisset Family Estates purchased the winery and embraced the rich heritage that the Count began so long ago. They even make a wine called The Count, which is blend of their reds.

Jacob Gundlach was another pioneer who was inspired by Haraszthy, and on March 12, 1858, he purchased four hundred acres in the town of Sonoma and called it Rhinefarm. He didn't begin planting his vines until 1859, when he returned from Bavaria, Germany, where he married his childhood sweetheart. He along with three partners—Dresel, Kuchel and Lutgens—planted sixty thousand vines on their ranch. By 1861, J. Gundlach and Company had begun producing and selling wine and brandy from locally grown grapes at their San Francisco location. In 1868, Charles Bundschu, from Mannheim, Germany, joined the winery. According to Gundlach Bundschu's history, "When phylloxera began devastating the vineyards in the 1870s, Gundlach and his partner, Julius Dresel, began experimenting with native rootstock Dresel brought from Texas."

The 1906 earthquake devastated their business because they produced and stored the wine in San Francisco. The ensuing fires destroyed one million gallons of wine and three family homes, so they headed to Rhinefarm to rebuild their business. Charles Bundschu died in 1910 from an illness he contracted during the 1906 tragedy, and his sons, Walter and Carl, ran the

Gundlach Bundschu ad, 1893. This 1893 ad shows Charles Gundlach, who joined the business in 1868, along with his son, Carl Gundlach, as vice-president. By this time, they were selling and distributing their wine and brandy all over America. *Courtesy of Sherry Monahan.*

business. The winery once again flourished until prohibition took place in 1920 and forced them to liquidate their company. They managed to hold on to 130 acres, where Walter and Carl continued to grow grapes for grape juice. When prohibition was repealed in 1933, the Gundlach Bundshu winery remained locked because their mother was a prohibitionist. Carl soon found a job in the winery business when Gustave Niebaum's widow hired him to run the Inglenook winery in Napa. Carl went back to the family business when his brother Walter died, and they sold grapes to many local wineries. In 1973, Gundlach Bundschu was bottling and selling its wine again. Today, the family still runs the business.

In 1854, General William Tecumseh Sherman and General "Fightin' Joe" Hooker planted grapes on their land but only kept it a few years. They sold their property to Albert M. Hay and John Q. McKenzie, who had lived on and farmed the land. On November 23, 1863, Virginia-born George Washington Whitman purchased it and began his winery. According to the 1870 census, George was sixty-six years old and listed his occupation as "wine grower." He was married to Nancy and had a son named Henry, who was living with his parents, along with his wife, Ada, and their daughter, Lillie. By 1876, Whitman's vineyard was producing fifty thousand gallons of brandy and had $7,000 worth of pipes and tanks. In 1880, he reported that he had 212 acres, of which 100 were vineyards, and in 1879, they produced forty-three thousand gallons of wine. At age seventy, he sold his property in 1883 to Eli T. Sheppard, who was a former consul to China and became the secretary of the Glen Ellen Viticultural Society in 1885.

Eli Sheppard named the winery Madrone and in 1887 constructed the first of two wine cellars. Because of poor health, Sheppard sold Madrone to U.S. senator George Hearst in 1888. Following the first epidemic of phylloxera, the vineyard was replanted by Hearst, who was a mining magnet and the father of publisher William Randolph Hearst. The sale included 400 acres, including a winery, a distillery, a wine cellar and eighty thousand gallons of wine and brandy, all for $80,000. They added plantings of Medoc and Gironde grapes to the vineyard, and in 1891, they had 150 acres of fruit-producing vines that included Zinfandel, Semillon and Mataro. Hearst's widow eventually sold the vineyard to the California Wine Association in the early 1900s, and the vineyard produced grapes for the CWA until the passage of the Volstead Act and prohibition.

In 1934, the property was purchased by the sausage-making Parducci family and was part of the estate vineyards of the early Valley of the Moon

Madrone winery, circa late 1800s. From 1941 to 1956, Enrico Parducci and Peter Domenici ran the winery and vineyard. The Parducci family continued to produce wines until 1997, when they sold it. *Courtesy of Valley of the Moon Winery.*

Winery. In 1953, when relations between the Parducci family and their business partners, the Domenici family, became acrimonious, the vineyard was split. The Parduccis took a smaller parcel of land with the winery, while the Domenicis took 152 acres of what was then known as Madrone Ranch. In 2005, the Domenicis sold the property. Today, that 152-acre vineyard is cared for by the father-son team of Joel and Morgan Peterson. Even though the Bedrock Wine Company is not open to the public, you can still taste history in a bottle with its Bedrock Heirloom Wine, which is made with 120-year-old vines from the Bedrock Vineyard.

Another portion of the original Madrone vineyard is managed by the current Valley of the Moon Winery. It currently uses the original winery cellar constructed Mr. Eli T. Sheppard in 1887. The Parducci family continued to produce wines at Valley of the Moon until March 1997, when neighboring Kenwood Vineyards/F. Korbel and Bros. purchased it. Today, Valley of the Moon Winery is owned by longtime vintners and good friends Dan Zepponi and Tony Stewart.

The last portion of the old Madrone vineyard, which contains six acres of Zinfandel, is managed by Joel Peterson of Ravenswood Winery. Its current vineyard dates back to sometime before 1892, when the Barricia

Vineyard was planted. However, the land dates back to General Mariano Vallejo, who traded it to his children's music teacher in exchange for music lessons. In 1978, Barbara Olesen and Patricia Herron bought the vineyard and named it Barricia by combining their own first names. In 2006, Pat decided to sell the winery since she was alone after Barbara passed; she had also recently turned eighty. Mel and Angela Dagovich bought the vineyard and still own it today. Ravenswood Winery currently makes a Barricia Zinfandel with the grapes.

Svente Parker Hallengren was born in Stockholm in 1836. He was a blacksmith by trade but raised sheep and grew grapes where he homesteaded in the Dry Creek Valley when he arrived in 1856. It wasn't until 1884 when he first planted vines in the Rockpile region of the Dry Creek Valley and produced wine from them, but he shipped all the wine he made back to Sweden. According to his great-great-great-grandson and current winemaker Clay Mauritson, "From what we understand, it was not a successful venture, so he stuck to growing grapes and raising sheep." According to the California Board of State Viticultural Commissioners' report in 1893, Hallengren had twenty acres of seven-year-old vines in Geyersville and produced fifty tons. The report noted that it was his first crop. Today, the family carries on Svente's heritage at Mauritson Winery in Healdsburg, with one exception: they sell their wine to everyone. Clay also said, "Our most sought after wines come from our Rockpile property, which is part of the original homestead."

Italian winemaker Giuseppe Simi was born in August 1830 and left his native Italy in 1849 determined to find gold in California. Sadly, his golden dreams did not "pan" out. By 1862, his brother, Pietro, had a liquor business and a billiard table in San Francisco—likely a saloon. In 1863, Giuseppe was assessed a license and tax fee of ten dollars to be a peddler, second-class, in San Francisco. His brother, Pietro, was assessed a license and tax of twenty dollars for selling retail liquors and being a dealer, and by the end of 1864, he was listed as having a billiard table only. In 1876, he and Pietro produced their first wines under the Simi name; ten years later, Giuseppe became a citizen of the United States. In 1890, they harvested their first crop at the stone wine cellar in Healdsburg, which is where the Simi Winery remains to this day. According to the California Board of State Viticultural Commissioners in 1893, the Simi brothers had 126 acres with three hundred tons of grapes and 150,000 gallons of wine. In June 1900, Giuseppe was going by the name Joseph, had been married to Nicoletta for thirty years, had two sons named

Louis and August and had two daughters named Isabelle and Elvira. Brother Pietro kept the retail liquor business in San Francisco, had also been married to his wife, Victoria, for thirty years, had a son named Harry and three daughters. On July 19, 1904, the *San Francisco Call* reported that Pietro had died suddenly but gave no other details. A little less than a month after that, on August 13, 1904, Giuseppe died.

At eighteen, the wise Isabelle insisted on expanding the cellars and reinforcing them with steel bars in the event of an earthquake. Two years later, the 1906 earthquake nearly destroyed San Francisco but left the Simi cellars untouched. In 1908, Isabelle traveled the country to visit distributors and promote Simi wines, and she married Frederick Russell Haigh, who was a bank clerk. Two years later, her mother passed away. A note about Nicoletta's death in the local paper claimed

Isabelle Simi. In 1904, Giuseppe Simi's oldest daughter, Isabelle, was crowned Queen of the Healdsburg Floral Festival and took over the family winery. *Courtesy of Simi Winery.*

that she was a wealthy vineyardist and winemaker largely interested in the Simi Wine Company of San Francisco and Healdsburg.

When prohibition began, Isabelle was forced to sell a portion of her vineyard holdings in order to keep possession of her cellared wine. She was banking on a quick repeal, but that didn't happen. Thirteen years later, in

Montepulciano Winery (Simi). In 1934, Isabelle established Simi's first tasting room, which was made from a twenty-five-thousand-gallon cask. It was placed in front of the stone cellars, and visitors walked through the doors that been cut into it. *Courtesy of Simi Winery.*

Isabelle Simi in the tasting room. Isabelle loved to greet visitors and enjoyed pouring wine for her guests. *Courtesy of Simi Winery.*

1933, Isabelle's winery business was ready to sell more than 500,000 cases of perfectly aged wine to a very thirsty public. Isabelle Victoria was born on September 4, 1886, and at the age of eighty-four, she sold the winery. She passed away on October 16, 1981. Even though the Simi family no longer owns the winery, you can still visit the historic winery that they built so long ago.

BAKED PASTA WITH FRESH MOZZARELLA

*1 lb. pasta, such as fusilli, campanelle or something with
plenty of twists and turns to hold cheese
1 tbsp. butter
1 tbsp. olive oil
1 lb. uncooked turkey sausage
½ large onion, diced
2 large portabella mushroom caps, finely chopped
4 cloves garlic, minced
½ tsp. oregano
1 tsp. red pepper flakes
½ c. Simi Cabernet Sauvignon
1 28-oz. can of crushed San Marzano tomatoes
1 c. Parmesan cheese
1 15-oz. container of ricotta cheese, low moisture
½ c. parsley
½ c. pasta cooking water
½ lb. fresh mozzarella, not packed in water, sliced in ½" slices*

Preheat oven to 425 degrees F. Bring large pot of water to a boil for pasta. Butter a 9" x 12" casserole dish. For individual portions, use 1-cup ramekins, about a dozen. Over medium heat, add 1 tbsp. olive oil to a large skillet. Remove sausage from casing and cook in skillet, breaking up into tiny crumbles with a wooden spoon until cooked through, about 7 minutes. Remove from pan and set aside. Add onions and mushrooms to the pan and cook until translucent and broken down. Do not crowd the pan. If this happens, first sauté the mushrooms and then add the onion. Salt and pepper to taste. Add garlic and cook for 1 minute until fragrant. Add oregano and red pepper flakes and season with salt and pepper again. Add wine and allow to cook until reduced to about half. Add tomatoes and bring to a simmer. Remove from heat. Salt pasta water and add pasta, cooking until al dente (about one minute less than package instructions). Combine Parmesan, ricotta, parsley, sausage and pasta water with al dente pasta. Drizzle about ½ cup of tomato sauce on bottom of casserole dish and pour pasta over sauce. Cover with another layer of sauce and slices of fresh mozzarella cheese. Bake for 15 minutes until cooked through, and for an extra crispy top, place under broiler for last minute. Allow to cool for 5 minutes and serve with simple salad or Italian bread. Serves 10–12. Serve with Simi Cabernet Sauvignon.

Recipe courtesy of Simi Winery.

In 1877, Zinfandel vines were planted along Sausal Creek. It wouldn't be until the early twentieth century when wine would once again be made from those grapes. In 1901, Manuel Demostene, a native of Genoa, Italy, began work on a ranch in the valley. Soon thereafter, another Italian immigrant, named Abele Ferrari, accepted work at the Italian Swiss Agricultural Colony in nearby Asti. Though prohibition crippled the wine industry, it allowed Ferrari to take advantage of declining property values, and he seized the opportunity to purchase Soda Rock Ranch and Winery in the Alexander Valley in 1923. After the repeal of prohibition in 1933, he completely rebuilt the old stone winery. In 1936, Manuel Demostene's son, Leo, married Abele Ferrari's daughter, Rose. The young couple established their new home at Soda Rock Winery, where Leo took over duties as winemaker.

Leo's dream of having his own winery became a reality in 1956 when he and Rose purchased Sausal Ranch, a 125-acre property that included Zinfandel grapes, of which many were established before 1877. Just recently, the Duncan family of Silver Oak Cellars purchased this unique property and is proud to be the stewards of these historic Zinfandel vines.

Geyser Peak, 1900. In the 1890s, founder Augustus Quitzow moved to San Francisco and was in the running to be a judge in 1894 on the People's Party ticket; he got one vote. *Courtesy of Sonoma County Library.*

Geyser Peak can trace its lineage back to German immigrant Augustus Quitzow, who planted his vines in 1880 in Geyserville. Tragedy struck in early December when his wine house burned to the ground. Luckily for him, he had insurance, which covered all but $2,000 of his $8,000 loss. It was rebuilt in 1882 and was perched on a hillside across from Geyser Peak Mountain. By 1882, the winery was back in business, but in early 1886, he filed an insolvency petition because he had debts of about $4,500. His creditors included the well-known wine men Kohler and Frohling. At Geyser Peak, you can still experience the history that Quitzow began back in the 1880s.

The Monte Rosso Vineyard is said to be one of the most highly regarded grape growing sites in Sonoma County California, and it is certainly historic. The vineyard was purchased by partners Benjamin Dreyfus and Emmanuel Goldstein in 1880 and named Mount Pisgah Vineyard. Before it could be planted, laborers cleared a tremendous amount of rock and vegetation. The first plantings succumbed to phylloxera, and the vineyard was replanted in 1890 with Zinfandel, the oldest vines on the property today.

When Benjamin Dreyfus passed away in 1886, Emmanuel Goldstein renamed the property Goldstein Ranch and built the stone gravity-flow winery that still stands today. The winery operated from 1886 until the start of prohibition and has not operated since. While it was originally planted in 1880, the vineyard fell victim to phylloxera and was replanted in 1890 with Zinfandel vines, which persist in meandering up the slopes today. However, Goldstein maintained production in the vineyards during prohibition, shipping harvested fruit to San Francisco for home winemakers. Goldstein's vineyard was among the few to survive prohibition intact, and once the law was repealed, he began selling his grapes commercially again. One of Goldstein's loyal customers was an Italian immigrant, Louis M. Martini, with a winery under construction in the heart of Napa Valley.

Goldstein Ranch was put up for sale in 1938 by Goldstein's heirs, and Louis M. Martini, concerned that he would no longer be able to source fruit from the vineyard, purchased it immediately. He aptly renamed it Monte Rosso Vineyard for its mountaintop location and rich red soil.

When Louis M. Martini acquired the ranch, the vineyards covered about 180 acres and were mostly Zinfandel. Louis M. Martini introduced Cabernet Sauvignon to the property in 1938, and these original vines

Louis M. Martini, 1933. Louis Martini was born in about 1888 in Italy and came to America in 1900. Before buying Monte Rosso, he was a "grape manufacturer" in Fresno, where he lived with wife Assunta, son Louis and daughter Lina. *Courtesy of Louis M. Marini Winery.*

continue to produce to this day. By 1940, the Martinis had planted up to 250 acres and knew that Cabernet Sauvignon and Zinfandel were the most promising varietals. The family farmed the steep terraces with surplus U.S. Army vehicles that they bought after World War II; these can still be seen on the property.

Today, the Monte Rosso Vineyard appears timeless, with the original three-story stone winery built in 1886 and the Victorian farmhouse built in 1903. Several blocks of old-vine Cabernet Sauvignon and Zinfandel twine up the slopes, with the entire Sonoma Valley sprawled below and San Francisco visible in the distance. Most importantly, Michael Martini, third-generation winemaker, can be found tending the old vines in anticipation of continuing the Martini tradition of blending rich, distinctive and memorable wines.

In 1881, a man named Andrea Sbarboro changed the Alexander Valley when he established the Italian Swiss Agricultural Association. He was born in Genoa, Italy, in 1839 and immigrated to San Francisco when he was thirteen. He worked for twenty years in his brother's grocery before establishing his own store. He and his associates began the colony with a membership of one hundred persons. Each member contributed $1 per month per share they owned to a general fund—a land-ownership cooperative similar to a mutual savings and loan society. Some of the shares were reserved for the soon-to-be-hired vineyard workers. As soon as the fund hit $10,000, the 1,500-acre Truett sheep ranch was purchased on November 8, 1881, for $25,000. The location was on the line of the San Francisco and Pacific Railroad, which made it perfect for shipping wine since they had a warehouse in San Francisco. The station was named Asti after a wine region in the Piedmonte province of Northern Italy.

Each worker was required to purchase a minimum of five but not more than fifty shares. When the prospective workers refused to comply with the mandatory purchase of shares, the cooperative plan was abandoned, and the association became the Italian Swiss Agricultural Colony. It became a commercial venture whose membership was restricted to Italian or Swiss immigrants who had either filed for or attained American citizenship. Even though the Swiss were allowed to join, not one did. The workers received monthly compensation, but it was put into a fund for two years until their "contract" was up. They bought items from a company store where they got what they needed and lived on the property. It was hoped that when their time was up they would use the money to start a business in the area.

The Italian Swiss Agricultural Colony had the distinction of having one of the first, if not the first, tasting rooms in Sonoma. Its founder, Andrea Sbarboro, rented train engines and cars to bring visitors to Asti, and their visits began with a tour of the winery, followed by tastings, lunch and more wine. These visits began in the 1890s but escalated after 1902 when he built the Villa Pompeii, which was designed to host guests who came to taste, tour and experience the wines and associated lifestyle of the Italian Swiss Agricultural Colony. When the 1906 earthquake rocked San Francisco, its effects were felt all over, including at Asti. Its large underground tank, which held red wine, cracked, and the Russian River was said to have flowed red.

Italian Swiss Colony. In 1898, the colony had the largest underground wine tank in the world. It even held parties there. *Courtesy of Asti Winery, Treasury Wine Estates.*

Italian Swiss Colony, harvest wagon, circa late 1800s. By 1889, the colony had cleared seven hundred acres, which were planted with mostly Zinfandel, Riesling and Charbonneau grapevines. They had also planted several varietals from Northern Italy. *Courtesy of Asti Winery, Treasury Wine Estates.*

In 1911, the Italian Swiss Agricultural Colony shocked the wine world when it won the Grand Prix medal for its Golden State Extra Dry Champagne during the 1911 Wine Exposition in Turin, Italy. It won the Grand Prix again in 1913 at the same exposition, but in Belgium. By 1915, it had won four Grand Prix awards, with the last for its Tipo Red and Asti Rouge, which was a sparking Burgundy.

Jeff Collins currently manages the Asti Winery, which is the old Italian Swiss Agricultural Colony. He said, "The son of Edmund Rossi (Asti chief winemaker and part owner at the time) told me personally of how, right as Prohibition ended, some folks wandered into the winery office and lab area and asked if they could taste some of the wines. Edmund grabbed a card table and some chairs, and they all sat down to taste. Immediately thereafter, they re-opened a true tasting room to the public." The winery managed to survive prohibition because it made sacramental wine and juice concentrate, which was sent along with a packet of yeast. It included instructions on what *not* to do to make wine. Even though you can't visit the winery at this time, you can still sample wine that's bottled at this historic winery. It produces Cellar No 8 and Souverain wines, which can be found just about anywhere.

Francis and Joseph Korbel left their native Prague, Bohemia, now part of Czechoslovakia, to escape political unrest. Their younger brother, Anton, arrived about ten years later. Francis was born on June 24, 1831, in Bohemia, Austria, and arrived in America on the SS *Columbia* in November 1850. Anton was born on August 26, 1841, and arrived in America in 1858. Joseph was born in March 1844. They arrived in San Francisco in the early 1860s, and there F. Korbel and Bros. began a manufacturing business that produced materials for the building industry. In the late 1860s, the Korbel Cigar Box Factory in San Francisco was established. In 1869, Francis was appointed as acting attorney for a San Francisco businessman named Julius Morris while he was out of town. In 1880, Joseph and Francis were the owners of a cigar box factory and living with their families in San Francisco. Their primary business in 1876 was printing lithographic labels for cigar boxes. Joseph, however, also founded a newspaper called the *Wasp*, and during its first two decades, the *Wasp* had a series of owners of various political persuasions and twelve editors.

During the 1870s, the Korbels raised prunes, beets, wheat and corn and ran a commercial dairy in the Russian River Valley. In 1883, they acquired the Arcata and Mad River Railroad, which was extended up the North Fork Mad River, where they built the Humboldt Lumber Company sawmill

Korbel brothers. Joseph (left) was married to Karolin and had two daughters, Caroline and Helena. They lived with older brother Francis (right) and his wife, Anna. Their younger brother, Anton (center), arrived in about 1868, which was about ten years after they first arrived. *Courtesy of F. Korbel Bros.*

around the same time. The town was originally called North Fork, but in 1891, it was renamed Korbel when the post office was opened.

The Korbel brothers entered the wine business in the early 1880s and experimented with several grape varieties, including Pinot Noir. Despite Pinot Noir being unusual for California's vineyards, the Korbels chose to work with them. As their wine business grew throughout the 1880s, they sent for Prague winemaker Frank Hasek. In 1886, the governor gave Joseph a land patent of forty acres in Sonoma. After the debut of his champagne, Francis Korbel began producing his premium Korbel California brandy in 1889.

Korbel and Hasek experimented with the méthode champenoise, which is the traditional French method for making champagne, and by the 1890s, Korbel champagne was being shipped all over. In 1891, they had 175 acres of fruit-bearing vines that consisted of Zinfandel and a mixed blend and were finishing their new cellars. By the turn of the century, Korbel was known internationally and was winning awards. Francis was active in politics, and in 1892, he was appointed as consul for the Austro-Hungarian empire in San Francisco.

By 1896, Anton had socially risen through the ranks of the local Knights Templar and was in charge of the Humboldt Railroad. The following month, a major fire caused $40,000 worth of damage to the winery when two 16,000-gallon fermenting tanks exploded. The fire raged for three hours, and one-hundred-foot flames were seen shooting into the air. The fire was finally put out when the remaining tanks, which were filled with that year's vintage, were smashed. Since the tanks were on the third floor, the wine flowed down and eventually extinguished the fire. They lost a large press and 150,000 gallons of wine.

On February 25, 1900, Joseph died after a brief illness. The newspaper noted:

> *A member of the firm of F. Korbel & Bros., cigar-box manufacturers at 723 Bryant Street, passed away yesterday, after a short illness, at the family residence, which adjoins their big mill. Deceased was one of the most important figures in the German colony of this city, a leading member of all the Germans societies, and one of the owners of one of the largest vineyards in the State. It is located at Korbel Station. Sonoma County, and has branches in San Francisco and Chicago. He also controlled a large lumber tract at Arcata, Humboldt County, which furnished material for the mills in operation in that county and in San Francisco.*

Later that year, Francis, Anton and their families were living next door to one another in San Francisco. Anton and his family, which included wife Therese and children Joseph, Martha, Elenora, Leo and Elsa, all lived with him.

In 1901, Francis saw an opportunity to utilize the many prunes growing on their land. He experimented for more than a year with making brandy from the prunes. The *San Jose Evening News* concluded, "He made a brandy which was fairly good, but which had neither cheapness of production nor any special quality." In 1902, F. Korbel and Bros. placed an unusual ad in the *San Francisco Call*: "LOST: ½ barrel of wine. Return to 723 Bryant St."

In 1903, Francis began selling many of his San Francisco–area properties to the business. Francis returned to his home in Prague in October 1908 and wrote on his passport application that he intended to return within two years. Anton and his wife also went to Prague, just two months after Francis and his wife did. They eventually returned to California, but then again in February 1917, Francis returned to Prague, stating that he would return as soon as his health permitted. He remained in Prague until his death on January 3, 1920, at the age of eighty-nine. His younger brother, Anton, was the last surviving brother of the three and passed away on February 6, 1925, in California.

Their winery survived prohibition because of the Korbels' diversified interests. Their children made sure that their fathers' hard work was not done in vain and continued to make méthode champenoise champagnes from the late 1930s to 1954. The surviving Korbels chose to sell the family business in 1954, but they were very specific on who the buyer would be. They wanted to preserve the legacy their fathers started and insisted that the buyer carry on the Korbel tradition of producing fine champagne by the méthode champenoise. They also insisted that the winery operate as a family and the company forever be known as Korbel Champagne Cellars. Adolf Heck bought Korbel and became the steward of the Korbel vision. His son, Gary, has followed his father's lead and carefully watches the Korbel legacy. Korbel still makes one of the champagnes that were made back when it all began, called Korbel Sec, but it's limited so you have to contact the winery to get it. In 1913, Korbel advertised, "Korbel Sec. The Sonoma County California Champagne… Delicious, bubbling, dry…It is made from genuine Petit Pinot grapes, bottled fermented…Quarts $1.85." You can also get the Korbel Brut, which Adolf Heck started producing in 1954 when he took over.

The Forchini Winery began in the late 1800s and early 1900s when Augustino Lituanio planted the Russian River Valley with a field blend vineyard with mostly head-pruned, non-irrigated or dry-farmed Zinfandel vines. Dry-farming is a method that relies solely on yearly rainwater to irrigate the vineyard. The Italian Swiss Agricultural Colony was among the wineries that used his grapes to make wine. According to the Forchinis, "This historic ranch [Dry Creek Bench] of mixed old vines had a record of grape growing dating back to 1886. Re-planted to Cabernet Sauvignon, Petite Verdot, Cabernet Franc, Malbec, and new additions of Zinfandel with 2 acres of 50 year-old Carignane and 12 acres of 100 year-old Zinfandel still in production." You can sample its historic wine, which is the Zinfandel, Dry Creek Valley Proprietor's Reserve.

Frei Brothers Reserve is a winemaking story more than a century in the making. In 1890, Swiss immigrant Andrew Frei purchased the core of what is now Frei Ranch in Sonoma County's Dry Creek Valley. The superb stretch of land was already a vineyard, but Frei brought it to prominence when he built a winery that produced twenty thousand cases of wine annually by 1895. In 1903, Frei turned the winery over to his sons, Walter and Louis, who adopted the name Frei Brothers.

After the repeal of prohibition, the vineyards caught the eye of Julio Gallo, winemaker for the rapidly expanding E. and J. Gallo Winery. The Gallo family began buying grapes from Frei Ranch, eventually signing an agreement to purchase the estate's annual wine grape crop. When Andrew Frei's descendants retired in the late 1970s, the Gallo family purchased Frei Ranch, further developing the vineyard and the winery. Today, Frei Brothers Reserve carries on the rich legacy of both the home vineyard and Sonoma's celebrated appellations.

Prussian Charles Behler planted his Glen Ellen vineyards in about 1870 after he prospered as a cobbler during the gold rush of 1849. In 1880, he still considered himself a shoemaker rather than farmer or vineyardist. He and his wife, Anna, lived on the farm with their five children. Although Charles passed away on November 11, 1893, his son Ben kept up the vineyard and planted more vines until 1924. According to winemaker Peter Wellington, who tends the vineyards today:

> *I don't know what the original grapes were in 1870 and one can only guess they included Zinfandel, Mission, and other early California varieties. The 1892 planting was a grape named Lenoir or Vitis aestivalis, which is a native of Texas. It was then grafted to Zinfandel, Carignan, Syrah, Durif (aka "Petite Sirah"), Grenache, Mourvedre, Tempranillo, Mission, Sylvaner, Semillon, Muscadelle de Bordelais, etc. The subsequent plantings in 1904, 1912, and 1924 included Alicante Bouschet, Grand Noir de la Calmette, Petit Bouschet, Trousseau Gris, Monbadon, Palomino, Colombard and others we haven't identified. Wellington Vineyards uses the grapes from the old vines in separate bottlings of Zinfandel, Syrah, Grenache, Alicante Bouschet, and vintage, white and tawny ports.*

Edoardo and Angela Seghesio. Edoardo passed away in 1934, leaving the winery and all property to Angela. Angela and her sons—Arthur, Frank and Eugene—continued making wine and shipping via the railroad. With their hard-earned knowledge, they added vineyards when they could purchase them without debt. In 1949, they purchased a second winery facility in Healdsburg to enable them to keep up with the growing demand for their wines. *Courtesy of Seghesio Family Vineyards.*

In 1895, Italian immigrant Edoardo Seghesio planted his own vines in the Northern Alexander Valley. According to the winery:

The Seghesio story begins in 1886, when Edoardo departed his family's vineyards in Piedmont, Italy, for a new life in America. Like so many immigrants, he was drawn to Northern Sonoma County and the Italian Swiss Colony to follow his passion for winemaking. Edoardo quickly rose through the ranks to winemaker, yet he yearned for home. The Colony's manager repeatedly encouraged him to stay, and finally, it was the manager's niece and the opportunity to purchase land, that convinced Edoardo to remain. That young girl, Angela Vasconi, and Edoardo were married in 1893.

In 1895, they purchased a modest home in northern Alexander Valley, more for the surrounding 56 acres Edoardo recognized as ideal vineyard land than for the home itself. They planted the Home Ranch that year to what became the family's lifeline—Zinfandel. Edoardo remained at the Colony while building his own winery in the evenings after work. Upon its completion in 1902, the young couple began Seghesio Winery while raising their five children. In 1910, they acquired additional acreage surrounding the bustling train station in what was then the town of Chianti. Edoardo, appropriately, planted the 10 acres to the Chianti field blend of Sangiovese, Canaiolo Nero, Trebbiano and Malvasia. That vineyard, called Chianti Station, is North America's oldest planting of Sangiovese.

Seghesio was also affected by prohibition, but six months earlier, Edoardo was convinced that it wouldn't last more than a year. Seghesio Family Vineyards reported that "[h]e decided to purchase his former employer, the Italian Swiss Agricultural Colony. The Colony, with a 4 million-gallon capacity winery and its 1,100 acres of vineyards, was quite a value at $127,500. As Prohibition prevailed, however, the debt was too much for Edoardo to bear. In 1920, he brought on partners: his brother-in-law, Enrico Prati, and the Rossi Family, who were previous owners and at whose request Edoardo came to America. Edoardo sold his shares in 1933."

When prohibition was repealed, the family once again opened the doors of the winery. Today, you can still enjoy wine from the original 1895 vines that Edoardo planted—look for its wine called Our Home Ranch Zinfandel. Another option is Chianti Station, a Sangiovese blend from what remains of the Chianti Station vineyard planted in 1910.

Seghesio Cellars. In January 1958, newspaper headlines announced that Sonoma County's wine industry had lost its matriarch when Angela passed away. Angela's legacy as an industry leader and a great chef lives on in her grandchildren. Her sons formed a partnership based on the ideals of their parents: family, hard work and passion for the industry. *Courtesy of Seghesio Family Vineyards.*

Seghesio Home Ranch. In 1895, the young couple purchased a modest home on fifty-six acres of prime vineyard land in northern Alexander Valley. The Home Ranch is planted to Zinfandel. *Courtesy of Seghesio Family Vineyards.*

RACHEL ANN SEGHESIO'S LASAGNA ALLA BOLOGNESE

FOR THE MEAT SAUCE
9 tbsp. onion, finely chopped
2 tbsp. oil
4 tbsp. butter
6 tbsp. celery, finely chopped
6 tbsp. carrots, finely chopped
8–10 ounces imported prosciutto, chopped
1½ lbs. ground chuck
½ lb. ground pork
1¾ c. white wine
3 c. whole milk
2 c. chicken broth
5 c. canned tomatoes, chopped

Cook chopped onion first in oil and butter. Then add celery and carrots. After it cooks together a while, add prosciutto, then sprinkle meat around the pan (turn up the heat a little). Add wine. Place the wine in the middle of the pan. Don't rush cooking. Add salt and pepper to taste. Make holes in the meat mixture with a wooden spoon so the liquid will be absorbed. Lower heat. Add 1½ cups of milk that has been warmed. Keep stirring.

Heat broth separately. After first half of milk has been absorbed, add the broth and the last part of the milk separately. Simmer and stir constantly. Then add the chopped tomatoes and simmer for at least 1 hour or longer. Note: You may cook lasagna while the sauce is cooking. Either make your own lasagna or use De Cecco brand. Lay out al dente lasagna on towels to cool.

BÉCHAMEL SAUCE

4 tbsp. butter
4 tbsp. flour
2½ c. whole milk
1 c. whipping cream
pinch of salt
nutmeg

In a heavy saucepan, melt butter. Stir in flour. Blend, then pour in milk and cream. Beat with a whisk and stir constantly until all is smooth. Then cook on a very low heat until sauce comes to a boil and thickens to a smooth cream sauce. Simmer, stirring 2–3 minutes. Remove from heat and season with salt and grated nutmeg. Set aside.

PROCEDURE FOR LAYERING

Choose a 14-inch bake-and-serve lasagna pan. Cover the bottom of the pan with a little bit of meat sauce, skimming it from the top, where there is more fat. Place a single layer of pasta in the pan. Spread enough sauce on the pasta to dot it with meat, then dot it with Béchamel and Parmesan cheese around the meat sauce.

Repeat layers: pasta, meat sauce, Béchamel, Parmesan four or five times. Final topping is meat sauce over lasagna strips, then Béchamel sauce and Parmesan cheese. Bake at 325 degrees until bubbly. Serves 10–12. Note: Total preparation takes about 2 hours. Lasagna can be made a day ahead and refrigerated overnight.

Recipe courtesy of Seghesio Family Vineyards.

ED'S EGGPLANT PARMESAN

TOMATO SAUCE
1 lb. sausage
½ c. fresh parsley, chopped
1 sprig fresh rosemary, minced
½ c. Seghesio Barbera
3 cloves garlic, pureed
1 medium onion, chopped
2 large cans of crushed or chopped tomatoes with juice

Using medium-high heat, sauté the sausage until almost cooked. Drain off almost all the fat, leaving some residual for flavor. Reduce to medium heat, add the fresh herbs and red wine to the sausage and continue cooking for about 5 minutes. Slowly stir in the pureed garlic and onion and sauté about 5 minutes. Add the crushed tomatoes and continue cooking until sauce reaches a slow boil. Reduce heat to simmer and continue to cook, adding salt and adjusting seasonvwings as needed.

EGGPLANT AND DISH PREPARATION
3 eggplant, peeled and sliced to ⅜" thickness
flour
vegetable oil
2 medium Mozzarella balls, sliced to ⅛" thickness
3 c. shredded Parmesan cheese

Preheat oven to 350 degrees. Salt both sides of the eggplant and place on paper towels for about half an hour to release excess water and bitterness. Lightly flour both sides of eggplant and fry in vegetable oil until golden brown. In a baking dish, layer the ingredients starting with the tomato sauce, then eggplant and topping with cheese. Repeat to make three layers, topping last layer with remaining cheese. Cover with foil and bake in oven for about 30 minutes or until bubbling.

Recipe courtesy of Seghesio Family Vineyards.

Foppiano Winery, dumping wine on August 15, 1926. During prohibition, federal treasury agents raided Foppiano Vineyards, forcing 100,000 gallons of wine to be dumped in a nearby creek. It became the most popular spot in town as the creek ran red with wine. *Courtesy of Foppiano Vineyards.*

Healdsburg was home to another Italian winemaker named Giovanni Foppiano. He arrived in New York from Genoa, Italy, in 1855 and traveled to California by way of Panama, where he walked the isthmus. He was looking for gold and eventually made his way to Sonoma County. After a few years, Giovanni's wife, Rosa, gave birth to the first of many boys: Louis A. Foppiano. Eventually, their family grew to have eight children. According to Louis, "In 1896, Giovanni purchased a working winery known as 'Riverside Farm' encompassing 80 acres, just south of Healdsburg. He established the Foppiano Wine Company and became an important supplier of bulk wine to Northern California customers. At this point, Louis A. joined the new family winemaking business and in 1910 took over the winery and all account deliveries to San Francisco's Italian North Beach neighborhood. He and his wife Mathilda also had Louis J. that same year."

When prohibition was enacted, Louis A. Foppiano was running the business. According to the Foppiano family, "To make ends meet during

Prohibition, Louis A. turned to farming grapes, shipping them to home winemakers in the western and eastern U.S. In addition, he grew prunes, apples and pears, all planted among the vines on the family ranch. Louis A. passed away in 1924, just two years before."

Once prohibition was repealed, the Foppiano Winery was ready to get back to making and selling its wine. The Foppiano family noted:

> *After Prohibition was repealed in 1933, the shrewd Louis J. was ready for business and began selling the 83,000 gallons of wine he illegally made in 1932. In 1941, Louis J. helped found the Wine Institute of California, a powerful organization that continues to give a voice to California wineries and grape growers. Louis J. served as one of its directors for 45 years and later that decade he started the Sonoma County Wine Growers' Association, whose purpose is to promote Sonoma County wine.*
>
> *[The year] 1945 saw Foppiano Wine Company become the second largest bottler of wine in Sonoma County, and Louis J. purchased the Sotoyome Vineyard & Winery, which adjoined the Foppiano property. The estate doubled in size to 200 acres. Louis M., son of Louis J. and Della, was born in 1947, followed by Rod Foppiano, father of current vineyard manager Paul Foppiano, and in 1949 a daughter, Susan, followed.*

Shortly after the Civil War, an Italian immigrant named Francesco Passalacqua arrived in California from San Lorenzo della Costa, Italy. He supported himself by selling produce from a vegetable wagon. According to the 1891 *Grape Growers and Wine Makers* report, Francesco had twenty acres of fruit-producing Zinfandel vines and produced twenty-five tons of grapes in Healdsburg. By 1896, Francesco had earned enough money to purchase a ranch in Alexander Valley for the cost of ten gold coins. Francesco and his son, Emil, planted Zinfandel grapes from those vines to make wine at the then family-owned Fitch Mountain Winery and Oliveto Winery. According to the owners of Dancing Lady Wines, "The wine that we produce today is made from the original Zinfandel vines planted by Francesco and Emil."

At the ages of nineteen and sixteen, Giuseppe Martinelli and Luisa Vellutini eloped from their small village in the Toscany region of Italy, making their way to California and looking for land to farm and start a winery. Giuseppe had been a winemaker in Italy, and with his viticultural

MARTINELLI POLENTA NONI ALMA STYLE
PAIRS GREAT WITH ZINFANDEL OR SYRAH

Regina Martinelli wrote, "This recipe is from my Noni Alma, my father's mother. My mom has been making it for our family for years. It's the regularly requested dinner for my brother's birthday. It's also my favorite meal during the cold, wet months to warm the bones."

1 lb. ground venison (you can also use hamburger)
1 lb. ground pork, optional Portuguese Hawaiian Seasoning
1 jar of Amy's Tomato Basil Sauce (or you can make your own tomato basil sauce)
1 c. red wine (Pinot Noir and Zinfandel work best)
1 bag of Golden Pheasant Polenta (it's the only polenta my Italian grandparents would ever use, and my mom swears by it)

Sauté the meat by itself until brown then put it in the food processor for finer meat pieces. Place the meat, tomato basil sauce and red wine in a saucepan and simmer for 2—4 hours—the longer the better. Optional: We make this the day before our family feast because when the meat can soak in the tomato and wine flavors, it's even more delicious.

Cook polenta as directed on the package and serve with the sauce on top...and Zinfandel or Syrah in your glass.

Recipe courtesy of the Martinelli Winery.

knowledge, he was hired to plant a vineyard for a farmer in Forestville. Within two years, he had earned enough money, and borrowed some from a local woodcutter, to purchase some land. In 1897, working side by side on a sixty-degree slope, Giuseppe and Luisa planted a small area of Zinfandel and Muscat Alexandria vines that later became known as the Jackass Hill Vineyard.

In 1918, Giuseppe died, leaving Luisa with four children and the farm to care for. Their youngest son, Leno, was twelve years old at the time and had wanted no other career in life than to be a farmer. Leno's two older brothers wanted nothing to do with the impossibly steep hillside, so after completing the eighth grade, Leno finished school and took on the sole responsibility of farming the Zinfandel vineyard. His family told him that only a jackass would farm a hill that steep. Hence, both he and his vineyard earned the name Jackass. Leno received all of his farming knowledge from his parents and through his own lifelong experience of tending the vines the way his father had. He even continued using a horse and plow until 1949. At the age of eighty-nine, Leno decided to hang up the keys to his John Deere and handed the vineyard over to his son, Lee Sr. Following the family tradition, Lee was introduced to vineyard work at the age of seven, performing all seasonal tasks necessary and learning the old viticultural practices handed down through the generations.

ASCENSION BY CHOCOLATE

16 oz. dark chocolate

9.7 oz. Scharffen Berger 62 percent dark (or other brand)

6 oz. Nestlé's semisweet morsels

1½ sticks butter

5 eggs, room temperature

1 c. sugar

Melt the chocolates and butter together in a sauce pan over low heat. Remove from heat when melted.

Meanwhile, beat the eggs and sugar together in a large bowl. Slowly add the melted chocolate and mix well.

Butter a 10" springform pan and line bottom with parchment paper. Pour in the mixture and bake at 350 for 30–45 minutes. Test with a knife. If it comes out clean, then it's done.

Recipe courtesy of the Martintelli family.

In 1900, Cesare Barbieri planted 27.5 acres of mostly Zinfandel that are now under the stewardship of the Gamba Estate Vineyard on the eastern edge of the beautiful Russian River Valley Appellation. The estate vineyard consists primarily of old-vine Zinfandel, as well as small separate blocks of Cabernet Sauvignon. The Gamba family still uses organic methods to counter any adversity faced in the vineyard, as it has been done since Cesare began it in 1900. Cesare sold the winery to Agostino Gamba Sr. in 1947, and according to the Gambas, "Agostino, Sr. and Elizabetta became good friends with the Barbieri's and the families enjoyed Italian-style family picnics on the property together. The Barbieri's continued working with Agostino Sr. for several years in the vineyard Mr. Barbieri planted a half century before."

Samuele Sebastiani was another Italian immigrant who planted roots in Sonoma County. In 1895, he left his native Tuscany region and arrived in the United States. His entered the wine industry just nine years later. He was a stonemason and quarry-mined the Sonoma hills for cobblestones used for building the streets of San Francisco. According to Sebastiani Vineyards and Winery, "He worked long hours and saved carefully to buy land in Sonoma County, from which he would make wine for the Sonoma community and San Francisco's restaurants. The winery was the only one in Sonoma County to continue operations through Prohibition, making a small amount of sacramental and medicinal wines. It has been joked, and perhaps with some grain of truth, that during this time there was a resurgence of people becoming very religious."

Samuele managed to survive both prohibition and the Great Depression because he built a skating rink, a motel, a theater and a meeting hall on the plaza at the Catholic church. The winery also noted:

> To keep people employed at the winery, Samuele began canning peaches, pears and nectarines. Shortly after Samuele's death in 1944, his son, August and his daughter Sylvia purchased the winery from the estate and began the expansion of the facilities and the product line, adding new varietal wines and proprietary blends. Always sporting his trademark bib overalls, August was recognized as one of America's most skilled and innovative winemakers of the time. August was also known for his tireless devotion to birds and their preservation—as evidenced by his lifelong support of Ducks Unlimited and his collection of rare doves and black swans. Today, Sebastiani Vineyards & Winery advances its record of acclaim under the guidance of vintner and entrepreneur Bill Foley, who acquired the winery in 2008.

QUICK MINESTRONE SOUP

11-oz. can red kidney beans

1 tsp. salt

½ tsp. garlic salt

1 clove garlic, pressed

¼ tsp. pepper

1 tbsp. oil

¼ c. chopped parsley

1 small zucchini, unpeeled and cut into small pieces

2 stalks celery, chopped

1 small carrot, diced

2 green onions, chopped

4–5 leaves Swiss chard, chopped

3 tbsp. butter

1 8-oz. can tomato sauce or 1 can solid packed tomatoes, mashed

2½ c. water

½ c. Sebastiani Chardonnay or other dry, white wine

¼ c. uncooked elbow macaroni, optional

grated Parmesan cheese

Place undrained beans in a large kettle or saucepan; mash about ⅔ of the beans and leave the rest whole. Add salt, garlic salt, pepper, oil and parsley, stirring well. Then add the vegetables, butter, tomato sauce and water. Simmer 1 hour or more, then add the wine. If used, add the macaroni. Simmer for an additional 10–15 minutes. If soup is too thick, add some water. Taste for seasoning and sprinkle with cheese.

Recipe courtesy of Mangiamo: The Sebastiani Family Cookbook
by Sylvia Sebastiani.

SEBASTIANI SPAGHETTI SAUCE

1 lb. ground beef, optional
1 tbsp. olive oil
4 tbsp. butter
4 stalks celery, chopped
4 onions, chopped
4 cloves garlic, finely chopped
¼ tsp. thyme
¼ tsp. rosemary
½ c. finely chopped flat leaf parsley
½ c. dried Italian mushrooms, soaked in a cup of hot water, then chopped
1 large can solid pack tomatoes, mashed with liquid
6 cans (8 oz.) tomato sauce
1½ c. water
1 c. Sebastiani Zinfandel or other dry red wine
1 tsp. sugar
salt and pepper to taste

If using meat, brown in olive oil and butter. Add celery and onions and cook until meat browns or they are tender. Add garlic and salt and pepper to taste. Add spices, mushrooms (with their liquid), tomatoes and tomato sauce. Fill tomato cans with the water and add with wine and sugar. Cook for three hours.

If using meat, a pot roast can be used. Brown the roast on all sides over medium heat in the oil and butter. Proceed as above and let roast simmer in the sauce for two hours. Remove, rest for 15 minutes and slice and serve as meat for your dinner.

Recipe courtesy of Mangiamo: The Sebastiani Family Cookbook
by Sylvia Sebastiani.

While the Kunde family didn't start making wine in Kenwood until 1904, the land has an older wine history. In 1879, James Shaw established his Wildwood Winery and, by 1891, had a total of two hundred acres in grapes, which included Cabernet. By 1893, Shaw was producing 100,000 gallons of wine at his Wildwood Winery.

Shaw's neighbor was a ship captain named James H. Drummond, and by the mid-1880s, Drummond had a very large collection of grapes, similar to the same quantity of Hamilton Crabb in Napa Valley. According to Viticultural Commissioner Charles Wetmore, his vines in 1883 included Franc Pinot, Pinot Mourad, Malbeck (Malbec) and Chardenai (Chardonnay). Drummond offered the first Cabernet Sauvignon varietal at a San Francisco viticultural convention in 1884. It's interesting to note that until this time, single-varietal wines were not the norm, except for Zinfandel. Most, if not all wines, were blends like Bordeaux, Sauterne, Burgundy and Claret.

In October 1887, Drummond advertised in the *San Francisco Bulletin*, "Vine Cuttings for Sale: All Varieties of Claret, Burgundy, Sauterne, and Rhine Wine Grapes. Also all the choice European Grapes." His sudden death in December 1889 ended his Dunfillan Winery. The *Sonoma Democrat* reported:

> *Captain J.H. Drummond, the well-known viticulturist of Glen Ellen, died very suddenly and unexpectedly at his home Friday morning, of heart disease. The deceased was a native of Ireland and 39y of age. He came to this county several years ago and at once engaged in the extensive and scientific cultivation of the grape. So successful was he in propagating and experimenting with the rare varieties that his vineyard became known abroad for the high quality and extensive variety of its vines. He rendered great service to the viticultural industry of the State by introducing new vines and demonstrating the adaptability of California soil and climate to their cultivation. A wife, who is at present in Monterey and several children survive him.*

Enter Charles Louis "Lou" Kunde, who was born on February 11, 1859, in Saxony, Germany, and arrived in America in 1882. He went to California in 1883 and he established a 2-acre fruit farm in Santa Rosa. He also had a 200-acre property in Geyserville where he grew grapes, prunes and cherries. The 1891 *Grape Growers, Wine Makers and Distillers* directory reported that Lou was noted for having 10 acres in grapes, mostly Zinfandel, in Windsor. In 1904, he purchased the Wildwood Vineyards from James Shaw. It included 650 acres and cost almost $40,000.

Lou Kunde. Kunde continued to produce Drummond's Cabernet Sauvignon as a single varietal, and at the Panama Pacific Exposition in 1915, it won a silver medal. Kunde also won golds for his Zinfandel and Burgundy. *Courtesy of Kunde Family Estate.*

In 1911, the Wildwood Winery made 100,000 gallons of wine, and Kunde sold at least 2,000 gallons of his 1910 vintage. Kunde's vines survived phylloxera because his Zinfandel vines, like all the others after during the 1880s, were grafted to St. George's rootstock. He also planned to survive prohibition by applying for a license to make nonbeverage wines for sacramental use. Sadly, Lou would not live to see his efforts, and while away visiting his sister in Germany, he was hit by a wagon and died in September 1922. His son, Arthur, took over the winery and managed to see it through prohibition. According to Jeff Kunde, "The Kunde family decided to close [the] winery in the late 40s due to the war, which created a worker shortage. In the following years more property was acquired and more vineyards planted, but all the grapes were sold the other wineries. Many award-winning wines were made from the Kunde vineyards." Kunde Family Estate was started in 1990 and was able to keep the original bond no. 202 from Wildwood Winery. It is run by members of the Kunde family.

PASTA VINO

1 medium yellow onion, chopped
2 to 3 tbsp. olive oil
4–5 sweet Italian sausages, skinned and crumbled
1 lb. sliced mushrooms
2 tbsp. chopped fresh basil
¼ c. dry red wine
2 c. canned Italian plum tomatoes, chopped
4 tbsp. milk
salt and freshly ground black pepper to taste
1 lb. rigatoni pasta
¾ c. grated Pecorino Romano cheese

In a saucepan over medium heat, sauté the onion in the olive oil until pale gold.

Add the sausages and sauté for a few minutes; add the mushrooms, basil and red wine. Allow the wine to evaporate, add the tomatoes and let the whole mixture simmer for 8 minutes. Add the milk, salt and pepper to taste and remove from the heat.

In a large pot, bring 4 quarts of water to boil and cook the rigatoni for approximately 12 minutes until just done. Drain and return the pasta to the pot. Add the sauce and combine. Sprinkle the Pecorino Romano cheese on the top. Makes 6 servings. Serve with Kunde 2009 Barbera.

Recipe courtesy of Marcia Kunde Mickelson of Kunde Family Estate.

HARVEST PEAR AND CARAMELIZED ONION
CROSTINI

1 sourdough baguette, sliced on the diagonal
2 tbsp. olive oil
3 tbsp. butter
3 medium sweet yellow onions
salt and pepper to taste
5 Comice pears washed, cut in half cored and cut into thin slices
1/3 c. balsamic vinegar
1/3 c. light brown sugar
1½ c. crumbled Gorgonzola or blue cheese
coarsely chopped toasted walnuts

Preheat broiler and line a large rimmed baking sheet with foil. Place sliced sourdough on your sheet and, using a pastry brush, swipe a bit of olive oil on each slice. Broil bread on one side until golden. Remove from oven. Turn oven to 425 degrees.

In a large fry pan, add all of the oil and 2 tbsp. of butter and heat until butter is melted. Add onions and cook until translucent, about 25 minutes. Remove onions into a bowl, add the remaining 1 tbsp. of butter and sauté pears for about 5 minutes until tender.

Add the balsamic vinegar and brown sugar together and add to the onions. Combine until mixed.

Place desired amount of Gorgonzola or blue cheese on crostini, then top with onions, followed by pear slices and walnuts, if desired. Put back into the 425-degree oven for about 4 minutes, remove and serve warm. Should make about 25 pieces. Serve with Kunde's Reserve Chardonnay.

Recipe courtesy of Marcia Kunde Mickelson of Kunde Family Estate.

Chapter 4

A BLEND OF OTHER PIONEERS

ALAMEDA COUNTY

Wrote Mrs. Frona Eunice Wait in her 1887 book *California Vines & Wines*:

> *Close on the heels of Napa and Sonoma Counties comes the Livermore Valley
> district in Alameda County. The geological formation of the valleys and slope
> of the Mount Diablo Range more nearly reproduce the soil conditions...of
> the Gironde in France than any other section on this coast...The fresh, saline
> atmosphere from the Pacific Ocean and Bay of San Francisco, tempered in
> varying degrees by altitude and proximity to the great interior basin of the
> San Joaquin, provides the golden mean between excessive moisture and aridity,
> while topographical features indicate the sections within this district where
> immunity from frost and flood may be enjoyed.*

Chateau Bellevue Winery was built in the mid-1880s by French engineer
Alexandre Duvall. Once he established his two-hundred-acre winery, he
sent for clippings from his native France. He and his wife, Rosa, had one
daughter, Amelia. At age nineteen, Amelia married against her father's
wishes to a man named Thaddeus M. Stevens in October 1894 in Livermore.
According to the newspapers, Stevens was a nurse in a sanitarium. Duvall
disowned his daughter, and she was believed to have fled to Chicago with
her husband. Sadly for Amelia, she was divorced by the time she turned

California vineyards. Beautiful California vineyards like these have survived phylloxera (twice), earthquakes and prohibition. It seems that nothing can stop them too long from producing delicious wine grapes. *Courtesy of Sherry Monahan.*

ROSEMARY ROASTED PORK LOIN
PAIRS WELL WITH A FULL-BODIED RED WINE

6 garlic cloves, minced
3 tbsp. olive oil
3 tbsp. fresh rosemary, chopped
1 tsp. salt
1 tsp. freshly ground black pepper
3 lb. boneless pork loin
1½ c. dry white wine

Preheat oven to 400. In a small bowl, combine garlic, rosemary, salt and pepper and mix well. Stir in the olive oil. Place the pork loin on a rack in a roasting pan. With the tip of a sharp knife, make 1-inch slits into the top and sides of the pork. Coat all sides with the rosemary mixture, pressing it into the slits. Place pan on the center oven rack and bake for about 40 minutes, until the internal temperature registers 145 on an instant-read thermometer.

Remove from oven, transfer to a cutting board and loosely cover with aluminum foil. Let rest for 10–15 minutes before slicing. Place the roasting pan over medium-high heat and add the wine, scraping the bottom and sides of the pan. Bring to a boil, stirring constantly. Decrease the heat and simmer for 10 minutes. To serve, cut the pork into ½-inch slices. Plate two to three slices and drizzle with the sauce.

Recipe courtesy of The Casual Vineyard Table, *by Carolyn Wente.*

thirty. She went home to live with her father, but he never forgave her, and she moved out eighteen months later. When Alexandre died in 1913, his estate was sold at auction because no one could locate Amelia. She was eventually located, but most of the estate, including 100,000 gallons of aged wine, was sold, with neighbor Charles Wetmore, acting for the coalition of wine merchants, buying most of it. Today, the Thomas Coyne Winery sits on a portion of Duvall's Chateau Bellevue.

Livermore resident Charles Wetmore opened his Cresta Blanca Winery in 1882. At about the same time, he became president and chief viticultural officer of the newly established California Board of State Viticultural Commission. Wetmore traveled to Europe and acquired cuttings from vineyards in the hopes of eliminating the poor reputation that California's wine industry was suffering. Upon his return, Wetmore offered these selections to California vintners, including Livermore resident Carl H. Wente.

Bonded Winery No. 876 was granted to Carl H. Wente, who partnered with Dr. Bush and began his Livermore winery in 1883, with Wente serving as manager. Wente was a German immigrant who purchased forty-eight acres of vineyard land in the Livermore Valley and named his winery C.H. Wente and Sons. He planted Chardonnay vines, or Pinot Chardonnay as it was known then, that Wetmore had obtained while he was in Meursault in Burgundy. By 1889, Wente had acquired more land, and fifty acres were devoted to French vines, which were about seven years old. The cellar had a capacity of fifty thousand gallons, with the bottling being done at the San Francisco office. At that time, the winery was making Claret and white wine.

Wente Family, circa 1895. *From left to right*: Ernest, May, Barbara, Herman, Carl H., Carolyn, Carl F. and Frieda (in the oven). *Courtesy of Wente Vineyards.*

In 1918, Carl's sons, Ernest and Herman, joined the business, with Ernest managing the vineyards and Herman acting as winemaker. At that time, the brothers changed the name to Wente Bros. Like a few others, Wente Vineyards survived prohibition by producing sacramental wines. Over the years, Ernest took a great interest in Chardonnay, continually upgraded each new planting and gained a reputation for having the finest Chardonnay vineyard in California. Ernest imported a number of varieties from Montpelier, and Chardonnay was one of the selections. In the 1940s and '50s, winegrowers throughout the state selected cuttings—now known as the pre–University of California at Davis "Old Wente" clone—from this vineyard. The Wente family eventually bought Wetmore's Cresta Blanca and today grows 850 acres of Chardonnay in the Livermore Valley and Arroyo Seco appellations. In addition to grapes, Wente has olive trees and makes olive oil from those fruits as well.

Green Beans with Caramelized Shallots, Bacon and Hazelnuts

1 lb. fresh green beans, stem ends trimmed
1 thick bacon strips, diced
4 shallots, quartered lengthwise
¼ c. toasted, chopped hazelnuts
salt and pepper to taste

Bring a large pot of salted water to a boil over high heat. Add the beans and cook until tender, 3–4 minutes. Drain. Heat a sauté pan over medium heat. Add the bacon and cook until the bacon becomes a little crispy, about 10 minutes. Remove the bacon from the pan and transfer to paper towels to drain. Add the shallots to the bacon fat, still over medium heat. Cook, stirring frequently until caramelized and golden brown, about 5 minutes. Drain off most of the fat, leaving 2 tbsp. Add the beans and cook until lightly browned, about 5 minutes. Add the bacon and hazelnuts, season with salt and pepper and mix well.

Recipe courtesy of The Casual Vineyard Table, *by Carolyn Wente.*

Left: James Concannon, 1875. The patriarch was born on St. Patrick's Day in 1847. He surely had the luck of the Irish with him! *Courtesy of the Concannon family.*

Opposite: James Concannon. John is the fourth-generation Concannon and the current winemaker. He noted, "In the late 1800s, James became one of the first to craft Bordeaux and Rhône-style wines in California." *Courtesy of the Concannon family.*

Another Livermore winemaker began his winery in 1883 as well. The Concannon family immigrated here in 1865 and landed in Boston before heading west. They arrived in San Francisco shortly after 1874, and they settled in the Mission district. James often conversed with Archbishop Alemany, who ran the Mission Dolores.

The archbishop sensed that James and his wife Helen weren't happy in San Francisco, so he said to James, "I know you have this family and want to improve yourself, so why don't you get some land and produce Sacramental wine for the Catholic Church." James did just that when he bought forty-seven acres in Livermore in 1883, and the Concannon family is still producing wine at the same location.

James's son, Joseph, guided the winery through prohibition, making sacramental altar wines for the archbishop of San Francisco. Joseph was affectionately known as "Captain Joe" due to his service in the First Cavalry under General John Pershing and Lieutenant George Patton. When Captain Joe completed his military service, he decided to come home, start a family

and take over the winery. Under Captain Joe's watch, Concannon hired the first professional female winemaker, replaced original vines that were lost to phylloxera and increased the acreage of the Concannon estate. By the 1960s, Grandson Joe oversaw the vineyards, and Grandson Jim headed up the winemaking.

The Concannons were the first Irish family to begin a successful winery, and they were also the first to bottle the Petite Sirah grape as a single varietal in 1961. The family shared their recipes for fisherman's chowder and Irish soda bread, which originated with the Concannon clan on the Aran Islands in Ireland. Enjoy the meal with a glass of Concannon Chardonnay. As they say in Ireland, "Sláinte!"

CONCANNON FISHERMAN'S CHOWDER

ALTER THE SEAFOOD WITH VARIETIES AVAILABLE IN YOUR SEAFOOD MARKET.

¼ c. diced pancetta

1 c. each diced onion, celery and carrot

1 bay leaf

1 tsp. fresh thyme leaves

2 c. fish or clam broth

1 lb. potatoes, peeled and cut into ½-inch chunks

½ tsp. salt

1 c. half and half

8 oz. skinless cod, halibut or other flakey white fish fillets, cut into 1½-inch chunks

8 large shrimp, peeled and deveined

8 evenly sized medium sea scallops, muscles removed

thyme sprigs for garnish

pepper or hot sauce

In soup pot, cook pancetta over medium-low heat until golden. Add onion, celery, carrot, bay leaf and thyme and cook, stirring, until tender, 10 minutes. Add broth and 2 cups of water and heat to boil. Add potatoes and salt; cook until tender, 15 minutes. Add half and half, fish, shrimp and scallops and cook, covered, without boiling, until cooked, 6 to 8 minutes. Ladle into bowls and garnish with thyme sprigs. Add pepper or hot sauce to taste. Serves 4–6.

Recipe courtesy of Concannon Vineyards.

CONCANNON IRISH SODA BREAD

2 c. milk

¼ c. plain low-fat yogurt

1 large egg

1 tbsp. honey

2½ c. whole wheat flour

2 c. unbleached flour

½ c. plus 1 tbsp. wheat germ

2 tsp. baking soda

1 tsp. salt

4 tbsp. cold butter, cut in small pieces

Heat oven to 350 degrees F. Lightly butter 9-inch springform pan. Whisk milk, yogurt, egg and honey in small bowl. Combine both flours, wheat germ, baking soda and salt in large bowl. Add butter and rub with fingertips to make coarse crumbs. Add milk mixture; stir to blend. With floured hands, mound in pan. Bake until tester comes out clean, 45–50 minutes. Cool in pan. Serves 8.

Recipe courtesy of Concannon Vineyards.

AMADOR COUNTY

Amador County is one of California's older wine areas, and the Deaver Vineyards in Plymouth has a rich history that dates back to its early days. According to the Deavers, their ancestors were lured by the promise of gold. In September 1853, Jacob Clark Deaver left Missouri and eventually settled in the Shenandoah Valley with his father, Jason McFarland Deaver, in 1859. In 1868, Jason purchased 160 acres.

Jacob married Matilda in 1871 in Amador County and had twelve children, one of whom was Grover Cleveland. Grover was a teacher, as was his wife, Amy Elizabeth. The couple had three children to raise, but when Grover suddenly died due to a heart attack in 1926, Elizabeth was left with three children to raise. It was Elizabeth's second marriage, to Joseph Davis in 1927, that combined two of Amador County's oldest families.

Joseph was the son of John James "JJ" Davis, who began his journey across the plains in 1848 to California from Ripley County, Indiana. In the midst of his journey, he stopped in Iowa to learn the cooper trade before continuing his journey to California. By 1852, JJ had settled in the mining town of Placerville, home of the "Hangtown Fry." In 1854, JJ planted his first vines (mission grapes). By 1869, he had his own cooper shop and his own vineyards and produced limited quantities of wine. According to family stories, by 1870, JJ had 117 acres. Today, 6 acres of his original mission grapes still remain in production in the Deaver family. Following the advice of his good friend and fellow vineyardist Adam Uhlinger, he began to plant Zinfandel.

Kenneth Isaac "Ken" Deaver was born in 1919 and was a rancher from the beginning. He tended to the family's ranch, which included cattle, sheep, pigs, peaches, apricots, plums, almonds, walnuts and grapes. Since the first plantings, the Davis-Deaver farm sold their grapes to home winemakers around the area. Ken continued that tradition as he tended each day to the two hundred acres that were left to him by Joseph Davis. In 1986, Ken Deaver bottled his first Zinfandel with the trademark Deaver label. They still make an old-vine Zinfandel from vines that Ken's great-grandfather planted on the original Deaver homestead in Shenandoah Valley in the 1860s.

Davis put his coopering skills to work and made wine barrels for his friend Adam Uhlinger. Uhlinger was born in Switzerland in about 1820 and lived in Fiddletown, Amador County, with his wife, Ursula, and their three adult sons. He and his sons ran the winery, which opened in 1856, until it was sold to Italian immigrant Enrico D'Agostini, who arrived in America in 1914. Enrico was born in Italy in 1888 and married Cathalina, and the couple had nine children. When they first arrived in America, they assumed American versions of their names, and in the 1920 census, Enrico is listed as "Henry" and Cathalina is shown as "Mary."

This Enrico should not be confused with the Enrico D'Agostini of Alameda, who married Jesusita Rea, the daughter of a wealthy Mexican don in Mazatlan. That Enrico came home drunk one night in 1916 and began beating his wife, so she shot him with a revolver. Our Enrico served in both World War I and II and remained in Plymouth until at least 1940.

The D'Agostini Winery is one of the oldest in the state and was purchased by the Sobon estate winery when Leon and Shirley Sobon bought each other a second winery for their thirtieth wedding anniversary

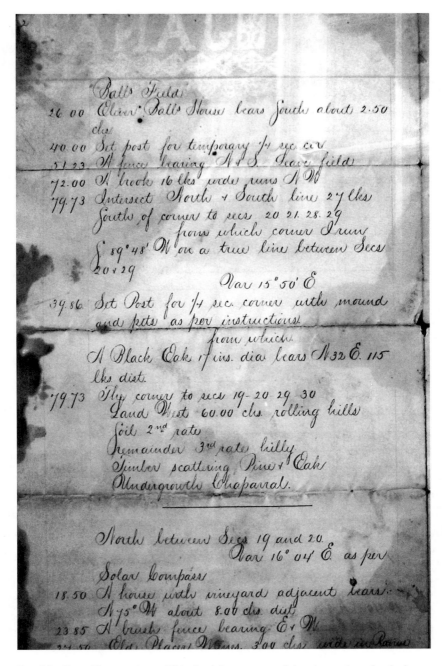

"Balls Field"

26.00 Clear Balls House bears South about 2.50 chs

40.00 Set post for temporary 1/4 sec cor

51.23 A fence bearing N & S. Leave field

72.00 A brook 16 lks wide runs N W

79.73 Intersect North & South line 27 lks South of corner to secs 20 21. 28. 29 from which corner I run S 89°48' W on a true line between Secs 20 & 29

Var 15°50' E

39.86 Set Post for 1/4 sec corner with mound and pits as per instructions

from which

A Black Oak 1 ins. dia bears N 32 E. 115 lks dist.

79.73 1/4 corner to secs 19-20 29 30 Land West 60.00 chs rolling hills Soil 2nd rate remainder 3rd rate hilly Timber scattering Pine & Oak Undergrowth Chaparral.

North between Secs 19 and 20. Var 16° 04 E as per Solar Compass

18.50 A house with vineyard adjacent bears N 75° W about 8.00 chs dist

23.85 A brush fence bearing E & W

27.50 Old Placer Mines 3.00 chs wide in Ravine

Deed for Scott Harvey winery. This deed shows some of the vineyards on land where the Scott Harvey winery sources its grapes. *Courtesy of Scott Harvey.*

present. The winery that Uhlinger began and D'Agostini continued has been designated as California State Historic Landmark No. 762. You can still taste history in a bottle by getting the Fiddletown Zinfandel, which is made with 1910 vines.

The vineyard in Sutter Creek where Scott Harvey Wines gets its grapes has only changed hands four times since it was planted in 1869. Scott said:

> *The land the vineyard is on was originally settled by the Upton family as a gold mining claim. The Upton family along with the neighboring Ruff family planted a Zinfandel vineyard that spanned across both their mining claims. Many vineyards were planted during this time to supply the thirsty miners of the thriving gold camps. A few still exist to this day. Some may be older and some younger, but Vineyard 1869 is the only one that has documentation proving its age. That is why we call it "America's Oldest Documented Zinfandel Vineyard." Back in the mid-1800s the new State of California set about establishing section corners on every square mile starting at Mt. Diablo in the San Francisco Bay area. By the time they got across the state to Amador County it was 1869. One of the documents recorded setting the section corners mentions this vineyard as a reference point. So we know the vineyard existed in 1869, but do not know how old it already was when the document was recorded.*
>
> *Once section corners were established, the State set about converting all the mining claims to deeded property. The original deed to this property was to Mahala Upton and was signed by Ulysses S. Grant as President. The property was 600 acres and the vineyard continued providing income for the Upton Family for many generations.*

The Upton family arrived in Shenandoah Valley in 1863, led by John Dale Upton, who was born in Illinois, and his wife, Mahala Teeter Upton, who was born in Virginia. According to Scott, Zinfandel and Black Saint Peter's vineyard nursery stock came from the East Coast in about 1850 to California. Both varieties came from Europe to the East Coast, and both varieties were planted in the vineyard they designate as Vineyard 1869. This ancient vineyard contains non-irrigated, stand-alone, head-pruned vines that fully express the Amador Zinfandel terroir. These historical vines are used to make an old-vine Zinfandel named, appropriately, Vineyard 1869.

Contra Costa County

Irishman James O'Hara and John Marsh planted vines in Oakley, California, in the 1890s. They hired Chinese workers to plant the earliest vines, and then the Italian, Portuguese and Spanish immigrants did more planting at a later date. Today, Cline Cellars uses grapes from the historic Oakley vineyard. It's home to its Ancient Vines wines, which are some of the oldest and rarest grapevines in California. They range from 80 to 120 years old and include 140 acres of varietals, including Mourvèdre, Carignane and Zinfandel. In addition to Cline, Bonny Doon Vineyard, Turley Wine Cellars and Bedrock Wine Company also use these grapes.

Lake County

Emilie Charlotte le Breton was better known as Lillie Langtry. She was born on October 13, 1853, on the Isle of Jersey, England, and was given the nickname "Jersey Lillie." She became a flamboyant British theater star during the Victorian era.

On her first visit, Lillie arrived in St. Helena in her lavish private Pullman railroad car called "Lalee," and then she embarked with a small fleet of stagecoaches carrying her entourage. Her paramour, Frederick "Freddie" Gebhard, already owned property in Middletown, Lake County, and after visiting him, she bought her land right next to his in 1888. She and Gebhard were never married because she could not get a divorce from her first husband, Irishman Edward Langtry, at the time. She and Edward were married in 1874 but had become estranged by 1881.

Lillie and Freddie chose not to live together but purchased adjoining ranches on the Guenoc property, where they lived for several years. Lillie purchased almost four thousand acres for $82,000. Freddie had been left a large sum of money from his merchant father and lavished Langtry with presents. Freddie eventually married someone else in 1894, but Louise Hollingsworth Morris soon divorced Freddie for another man. Langtry had filed for divorce in California in May 1896, but the divorce never occurred because Edward died in October 1897. Despite them both being free, she and Freddie never married. Lillie remarried in 1899 and became Mrs. Hugo Gerald de Bathe and, in 1907, the Lady de Bathe.

Above: Lake County vineyards. According to Slocum's 1881 book, *History of Napa and Lake Counties*, "Grapes do well here indeed, and much attention is just now being given to viniculture in this township…clearing off some 200 acres…for grape planting in 1882, with choice varieties of foreign table and wine grapes as well as the domestic varieties." *Courtesy of Sherry Monahan.*

Left: Lillie Langtry, 1882. Lillie was a well-known British actress who kept good company and even became a semiofficial mistress to the Prince of Wales, Queen Victoria's son Albert Edward ("Bertie"), the future king Edward VII. Among her friends were Irish writer Oscar Wilde and American artist James McNeill Whistler. *Courtesy of Library of Congress.*

Langtry made wine at her Guenoc Vineyards and proclaimed it the "greatest claret in the country." With the help of her winemaker Henri Descelles, she had fifty-one tons crushed for her first vintage and bottled wine in unique vessels portraying her likeness on the glass.

By 1900, Lake County wines were winning awards in international competition, and the region was earning a reputation for producing some of the world's greatest wines. Lillie sold the property in 1906, and the years of prohibition and vineyard destruction soon followed. It was a miracle that any vineyard area was left when the property was acquired by 1962. A Syrah, Petit Verdot and white grapevines of mysterious origin were found on the hillside vineyard site after at least half a century of neglect. In 1963, Malulani Investments acquired the twenty-three-thousand-acre Langtry estate and vineyards, with a focus of producing top-tier wines from the Guenoc Valley. The winery planted extensive vineyard acreage and was one of the first in California to plant the five major red Bordeaux grape varieties. The Langtry Red Wine is a true example of Langtry's artistry in blending the red Bordeaux varietals.

MENDOCINO COUNTY

While the Edmeades Winery in Philo is not historic, some of the wines it makes are. It makes a Zinfandel from the old Gianoli Ranch vineyard in Mendocino. The Gianoli family emigrated from Prata, Italy, in 1882 and homesteaded the Gianoli Ranch. They planted about twenty acres of Zinfandel grapes. Before prohibition, the wine would sell for forty cents per gallon, and that was delivered! During prohibition, the grapes were sold to Italian families who made their own wine in the Manchester area.

They also use Zinfandel grapes from the Perli vineyards, which were planted in the 1800s by Santo and Rosie Perli. Santo was born in Trento, Italy, in April 1855 and came to America in 1885. His wife, Rosa, immigrated in 1901 and the couple had a daughter named Carmella, who was born in 1905. By 1892, Santo was living in Fish Rock in Mendocino County, and he and his family lived there at least until 1910.

SAN DIEGO COUNTY

Five partners began the Bernardo Winery in 1889 on what was a Spanish land grant. They owned the winery until 1927, when Italian immigrant Vincent Rizzo bought the almost defunct winery from the partners. Vincent arrived in America in 1905 from Sicily. He kept the winery open during prohibition by making sacramental wine and grape juice guaranteed to ferment by the end of the road. The valley in which the winery is located was covered in vineyards—not a house was in sight—and the closest town was Escondido. Producing more than 150,000 gallons of wine in the late 1940s, the Bernardo Winery was a major wine supplier of San Diego County. The winery also produced cold pressed virgin olive oil from the many olive trees that were located on the property, supplying much of the tuna canneries in downtown San Diego.

SAN MATEO COUNTY

Vermont native Emmett Hawkins Rixford was an attorney by trade, but he was also a vineyardist. He was born in April 1841 and married Kate in 1875, and the couple had three children and lived in San Francisco. His brother, Gulian, also lived near him and was a member of the California State Horticultural Society in San Francisco. In 1880, he was noted as having sent samples of vines from the Fresno area that were thought to be infected with "Grapevine Krat." The California State Horticultural Society asked Justin P. Moore to make a presentation at its May 1880 meeting. Moore described it by saying that "[t]he disease...attacks the roots as well as the young shoots." It sounds like they were describing phylloxera but did not know it. In 1881, Emmett was appointed as a director of the California State Horticultural Society.

In 1883, Emmett wrote a book called *The Wine Press and the Cellar*, a manual for winemakers and cellar men. He explained the uses of foreign grapes and climates and gave explicit instructions on how to make wine. He noted that Mr. Craig was the first to plant a white foreign grape in 1867—it yielded 14.4 percent alcohol—and claimed that the first foreign red grape wasn't planted until 1867, by the Buena Vista Association. He based his findings on a report given by the Napa Wine Growers' Association in 1871. That report credited Mr. L. Goss as having been the first to plant Zinfandel in 1871, but other reports have found this is likely incorrect.

In 1884, Emmett planted a Cabernet (Margaux blend) vineyard on 37 acres in Woodside and named his ranch La Questa. In August 1886, he and his brother, Gulian, listed their property in Sonoma County, which was just two and a half miles west of the town of Sonoma. This property contained 320 acres, of which 50 were planted to healthy, bearing vines and 100 of oranges. Later that year, Emmett was appointed by the California State Horticultural Society to represent the association in Sacramento. By December, Emmett was the secretary of the Grape Growers' and Wine Makers' Association. In 1920, Emmett was still practicing law at the age of seventy-nine, while his son, Allan, was tending the vineyards. Emmett passed away on August 19, 1928, at the age of eighty-three.

Today, Woodside Vineyards still makes wine from the remaining three-quarters of an acre that Emmett Rixford planted in 1884. It also uses grapes from two acres of Zinfandel vines planted by John Hooper in 1894. According to founder Bob Mullen, "Our La Questa wine is only made when the grapes ripen enough, which isn't every year. Our label for that wine is very similar to that of the original La Questa."

SANTA BARBARA COUNTY

The Santa Barbara region was first planted by the Franciscans when they arrived there in the early 1800s. The Gypsy Canyon Ranch Vineyards and Winery in Lompoc uses grapes planted in 1887 by Dona Marcelina Feliz Dominguz. Another woman, Deborah Hall, is taking care of the dona's vines today. When she discovered the mission vines, she was advised to tear them out and plant new ones. She said, "I refused and thus still have the three acres of ancient vines from which I make the Angelica."

As for the exact details of the vineyard, she noted:

While there are no written records of the vineyard being planted I have gathered accounts from old timers. One remembers playing in the old vineyard as a young child. The little ranch house was built in the late 1800s, has a cellar, and we believe the vineyard was planted by the same family. When Prohibition hit, I believe the farmer let the vines get covered by the sage brush in order to hide them, hence they were forgotten till we stumbled upon them in 1997. We found them when we were scouting a place to plant the Pinot Noir and sent a sample to UC Davis for DNA testing. They confirmed they are ancient mission vines. We are just over the hill from the La Purisima Mission, so the cuttings most likely came from there.

The Historical Vineyard Society described Hall's Angelica wine as "Ancient Vine Angelica, this is a rich, hedonistically enjoyable wine, made from the Mission grape planted by the Spanish missionaries. It's very sweet and decadent, with tangerine, pineapple and apricot-infused crème brûlée flavors and a generous coating of spice that finishes in a honey-rich mouth feel."

SANTA CLARA COUNTY

In the late 1800s, Santa Clara was known as the "Valley of Hearts Delight" and was considered one of the most fertile valleys in California. It was planted with plums, apricots, cherries and nut orchards. Most importantly, it had many acres of wine grapes. In 1860, a farmer and grape grower named O. Webb reported to the *California Farmer and Journal of Useful Sciences* that he had planted 7,223 grapes, of which 3,000 were California grapes and 2,500 were White Muscatel. He also planted Black Hamburg, Burgundies, Malvoisie, Catawba, Malaga and St. Peter's in small quantities.

These fertile soils were the first to receive Black Burgundy from France by the hands of Pierre. The Mirassou family has been in Santa Clara County since 1854 and has been making wine ever since. According to Mirassou:

In 1854, Pierre Pellier, our great-great-great-grandfather, sailed from France with his bride, and his prized grape cuttings in search of the best California had to offer. Our family grew as Pellier's daughter married neighboring vintner Pierre Mirassou. The vineyards thrived and this fruitful partnership marked the start of more than a century of winegrowing in the area. Peter Mirassou guided the vineyard through the Prohibition years, choosing to continue cultivating the family vines. The demands for grapes for use in home winemaking and sacramental wine kept prices high, and after Prohibition's repeal the family winemaking business was revived.

Pierre Pellier, Mirassou winery. The first Mirassou generations worked together to build a thriving network of vineyards in the Santa Clara Valley that produced some of California's finest early wines. This rich family history and pioneering spirit have helped shape California winemaking and the emergence of the Central Coast as a premier growing region. *Courtesy of Mirassou family.*

Today, sixth-generation family member David Mirassou spreads the word of his family's wine heritage.

Just two years after Pellier planted his vineyard, another Frenchman named Adolph Siot planted his in Templeton. Siot eventually sold the vineyard to Joe Rotta in 1908. In the 1920s, Rotta then sold it to his brother, Clement Rotta, who bonded the winery after prohibition in the 1930s and forged the label into one best known for its hearty Zinfandels. Today, the Rotta label is being revived by one of their grandsons, Michael Giubbini, who remembered long, happy days of working in the vineyard as a child when he visited his grandparents from his home in Menlo Park. Giubbini undertook the task of replanting the old family vineyard. According to him, "Mostly to Zinfandel, it's a hearty grape that's proven in this area. I wanted everything head-pruned and dry-farmed the way my grandparents planted it."

The Novitiate Winery in Los Gatos was first built in 1888 by Northern Italian Jesuit fathers and brothers from the college at Mission Santa Clara (now Santa Clara University) as a means to fund their new seminary college built on the

Novitiate Winery, 1934. The name Novitiate simply translates to "house of the novices," the name used for seminary students. *Courtesy of Testarossa Winery.*

grounds the same year. For nearly one hundred years, the Jesuits made altar wines, as well as sweet, fortified wines at the Novitiate Winery.

Not surprisingly, the demand for church altar wine production skyrocketed during prohibition, and the winery and adjoining vineyards more than doubled in size during this period. With the repeal of prohibition, the winery continued to grow through the 1950s, as did the number of

Novitiate old cellars, 1895. The Novitiate Winery was best known for its famous fortified Black Muscat dessert wine (similar to a tawny port), which was a perennial gold medal winner at the annual California State Fair. *Courtesy of Testarossa Winery.*

students, who were also recruited to be volunteers in the vineyards and winery. By the late 1950s, more than 100,000 cases of Novitiate wine were produced at the winery. In 1986, the Jesuits shut down their Novitiate Winery brand, ending an amazing ninety-eight-year run. For the next ten years, the old winery was leased to other brands.

In 1997, Rob and Diana Jensen moved their existing Testarossa Winery into the historic Novitiate. Rob said, "The original 19th Century, three-floor, gravity-flow winery is still in use today to make Testarossa wines. However, the original structure is now mostly hidden from view by the many expansions the winery went through during the first half of the 20th Century." Today Testarossa is known for its collectable Pinot Noir and Chardonnay, but it keeps the historic legacy alive with "tasting room only" releases of Chardonnay, Pinot Noir, Rose and a "Brother Korte Cuvee" under the traditional Novitiate "black label."

Ridge Winery is a blend of four historic vineyards and wineries whose history begins in 1885 with Italian immigrant Osea Perrone, who was a San Francisco doctor from Northern Italy. He bought 180 acres near the top of Monte Bello Ridge, terraced the slopes and planted vineyards. The Monte Bello vineyard and winery was completed and bonded in time for the 1892 vintage, and the wine was transported to San Francisco, where it was bottled (and also sold from barrel) by the Montebello Wine Company. After Osea's death in 1912, ownership of the property passed to his nephew, also named Osea, who had worked on the ranch. Young Osea expanded the operation to more than 500 acres. He held on to the property during prohibition and, after repeal, restarted production. Perrone died in 1936, but limited production continued until 1943, when the winery closed and the last vineyards were abandoned. Ridge leased additional acreage from the Trentadues and planted Bordeaux varietals, ultimately buying those parcels in 1987. The historic winery is the heart of the present Monte Bello production facility.

Next was Pierre Klein, who was an Alsatian who came to California in 1875. He managed San Francisco's Occidental Hotel restaurant, where he championed the best of California wines. In 1888, he purchased 160 acres on Monte Bello Ridge (currently known as the Jimsomare Ranch). Determined to produce fine Claret in the style of the Médoc, he planted Bordeaux varieties on their own roots. In the early 1890s, he began selling his Mira Valle wines to several San Francisco restaurants. In 1895, he entered his wine in the Bordeaux Exposition, where he took an honorable mention. He won two gold medals at the Paris Exposition of 1900—one for his Claret, the other for his "Grand Vin," known as the "Château Lafitte of America." When phylloxera attacked his vines after the turn of the century, he did not replant and retired in 1910. He sold the property in 1913, and in 1936, it was purchased by the Schwabacher family of San Francisco, who renamed the property Jimsomare. Today, Ridge farms the original Klein property as part of its Monte Bello estate.

The third vineyard and winery to make up Ridge is the Torre Ranch. In 1890, John Torre, a successful Nevada cattle rancher, purchased one hundred acres on Monte Bello Ridge, planted vines and built a barn atop a cellar dug into the hillside. In 1908, John's nephew, Vincent, and wife, Dominica, arrived from Nevada to run the vineyards and winery at Monte Bello. They acquired the property upon John's death in 1913 and produced mostly Zinfandel, selling it for shipment by rail to New York. Prohibition closed the Torre winery in 1920, and the vines died out over time. Today, the oldest vines are those planted by

Chardonnay vines. These vines were in the early stages of growth in late April. *Courtesy of Sherry Monahan.*

William Short in 1949. The old Torre winery building now houses the Monte Bello tasting room and group facilities.

The last vineyard and winery that encompasses Ridge Winery is Rousten Ranch, which was bonded no. 180. Charles Rousten purchased seventy-five acres on Monte Bello in 1903. His property was just above Klein's and one mile below Torre. He planted vines and built a winery where he made his wine. During prohibition, he replanted most of the vines to prunes but kept about eight acres of vineyards. After repeal, he produced a little wine until his death in 1941, when his son, Charlie, inherited the property. Charlie operated the winery until sometime in the 1950s, when, fed up with the increasing paperwork demanded by the federal authorities, he famously refused to pay the federal excise tax on his wine. He dumped all the wine on the ground in front of a federal agent and threw him off the property. He tore out the remaining vines, closed the winery and focused on prunes, cattle and hay. When Charlie died in 1990, he left his land to Lois Ortmann. A high school teacher during the day, Lois developed a successful horse boarding operation on the ranch. In 2007, Lois signed a long-term lease with Ridge on thirty-seven acres, and new vines were planted starting in 2008.

Today, Ridge farms all four ranches, producing two red wines (Monte Bello and Estate Cabernet Sauvignon) and limited quantities of white wine (Monte Bello Chardonnay and Estate Chardonnay).

SAN JOAQUIN COUNTY

The Lodi appellation is located in this old county, and its wine history can be traced back to a captain named Charles M. Weber, who was probably the first to plant vines in the area in 1850. William West was likely the first person to start a commercial nursery in 1853. The main grapes grown in Lodi in the late 1800s were Tokay and Zinfandel. Other people soon followed, including Joseph Spenker, who arrived in Stockton in 1868 with twenty-seven cents in his pocket. By 1869, he owned more than one thousand acres in the Central Valley, including the ranch now called Jessie's Grove in Lodi. His great-granddaughter, Wanda Bechthold, said, "In 1885, great-grandfather met William West, a successful nurseryman who had started one of the first commercial wineries (El Pinal Winery) in California with his brother, George West. In 1885, West talked to Joseph about growing grapes and showed him all the different cuttings he had available. Joseph had heard good things about Cinsault, also known as Black Malvoisie, and in 1886, he planted his first twenty-five acres to this grape in the heart of the ranch." Joseph planted five acres of Zinfandel in 1889 and added more acres in subsequent years. Many of these vines remain in production today.

In 1870, he went to a wedding in Stockton, met a beautiful girl, Anna Schlieman, and married her the next day. They had two children, Jessie and Otto, who grew up in the home that Joseph built for his family in 1906. Upon the death of her father, Joseph, daughter Jessie took over and rejected all ideas of changing the Oak Grove. Jessie patterned her life in her father's noble footsteps and was a true pioneer of the San Joaquin Valley.

The historic vines that Spenker planted in 1885 are in Bechthold Vineyard, the oldest continuously farmed vineyard in the Lodi American Viticultural Area (AVA), consisting of twenty-five acres of gnarled head-trained vines. Bechthold Vineyard is actually part of the larger Spenker Vineyard property, with Jessie's Grove Winery sitting at its center. Wanda Bechthold, the great-granddaughter of Joseph Spenker, said, "While Joseph had already planted Cinsault, he also planted Madeline, Black Hamburg, Sweetwater, Black Ferra and Emperor, which were popular at the end of the nineteenth century." She added, "Part of his second planting, which is a field mix of mostly Zinfandel with Carignane, Mission, Tokay and a grape called Black Prince (a Black Muscat variant), is bottled by Jessie's Grove under the Royal Tee single vineyard designation." Other wineries using grapes for this historic vineyard include Bonny Doon Vineyard, Turley Wine Cellars and Michael-David Winery.

SAN LUIS OBISPO COUNTY

Saucelito Canyon Winery's story began in 1880, when three acres of Zinfandel vines were planted in the rugged terrain of the upper Arroyo Grande Valley on California's Central Coast. Today, it's called San Luis Obispo. Homesteader Henry Ditmas was an English expatriate and civil engineer who became a farmer. Along with his wife, Rosa, and their son, Cecil, he lived on the ranch. Henry planted Zinfandel and Muscat vines in addition to apple and pear trees in Saucelito Canyon in 1880. He used to the grapes make wine at Rancho Saucelito and at nearby St. Remy Winery.

Saucelito Canyon, 1894. Founder Henry Ditmas was born in England in about 1845 and lived in San Luis Obispo County. From 1877 to 1878, he served as postmaster in La Playa. *Courtesy of Saucelito Canyon Vineyard and Winery.*

The vines of Rancho Saucelito, named for the property's little willow trees called "sauce" in Spanish, survived prohibition and produced wine up until the early 1940s, after which they were abandoned in favor of dry land grazing. A new chapter was written one century later when Bill Greenough painstakingly restored the abandoned old vineyard and began making what has become one of California's most distinguished Zinfandels.

TEHAMA COUNTY

Peter Lassen has the distinction of being the first man to plant nonmission vines in Northern California. He planted his first acre of vines on his Rancho Los Bosquejo in 1844 in Vina, which is a town in Tehama County. He left his native Denmark in 1830 and headed for America, where he settled in Boston, Philadelphia and then Missouri. He stayed in Missouri until 1839

Peter Lassen. Lassen was born on October 31, 1800, at Farum, Denmark, a small village located fifteen miles from Copenhagen. *Courtesy of National Archives.*

and then headed for Oregon with a small emigrant party traveling west. From there, he made his way to the Russian Colony and then to John Sutter's ranch before settling in what is now Vina for a while. Lassen established the town of Benton City on his ranch, and in the summer of 1847, he returned to Missouri to recruit settlers for his new community. In the spring of 1848, he brought back a small group of emigrants, and they were the first to cross over the infamous Lassen Trail. When he returned, he discovered that the people who were already living there had deserted the town and left for Sutter's Mill due to the gold rush. In May 1850, Lassen sold half of his ranch to Joel Palmer to buy a steamer for the transportation of goods—he christened it the *Lady Washington*. Unfortunately, the ship sank, and Lassen was forced to sell the remainder of his ranch to German Henry Gerke. He propagated Lassen's one acre into one hundred acres and created his own wine called "Gerke," according to New Clairvaux.

Gerke eventually sold the ranch to his railroad baron friend Leland Stanford, who named it the Great Vina Ranch. By 1888, Stanford had turned Gerke's 100 acres into 3,000 and had the largest number in the entire area. In 1891, he had 3,705 acres, with more than 3 million wine-bearing grapes, which included Zinfandel, Trousseau, Burger and many other varieties. Ship captain Hamden W. McIntyre, who designed several wineries in Napa (including Inglenook), was the general manager at Vina for some time. Stanford died in 1893, but his wife, Jane, took over the winery. She made wine despite being a temperance advocate and was criticized by her peers for it. By 1915, with prohibition looming, she ordered all the vines be torn out and replaced with alfalfa.

The land was purchase in 1955 by the Abbey of New Clairvaux, which is a community of Trappist monks. Today, the monks make wine where the great Leland Stanford once did. According to New Clairvaux, "While we are the first Cistercian winery in the Americas, our order has a strong agricultural and winemaking foundation dating back to the 12th century in Europe. This tradition includes some of the finest vineyards in the world, such as Clos Vougeot in Burgundy and Kloster Eberbach in the Rheingau."

Chapter 5

HISTORIC VINES

Historic vineyards exist throughout California, and while these vineyards don't offer tours, you can still sample their wines. They grow grapes in the historic areas and then sell them to winemakers who, in turn, bottle and sell them.

Fiddletown, Amador County, is home to the 1865 Rinaldi Vineyard, which is head-trained and largely dry-farmed. Thirty-eight acres were originally planted to 95 percent Zinfandel, along with mission, White Muscat and Black Muscat, and there are still vines in the original 1865 block. While the vineyard was revitalized in 2000, there are various blocks at different ages since the 1950s. The total vineyard and ranch parcel is eighty-two acres. Both Rombauer Vineyards and Terre Rouge and Easton Wines use these vines to make wine.

Napa County is home to the historic R.W. Moore Vineyard, which has survived and has been productive for more than one hundred years. In 1883, a seventy-four-acre parcel of land containing the R.W. Moore Vineyard sold for $5,000, and the value had doubled to $10,000 by 1886. Phylloxera and a bad economy brought their combined effects to bear on Napa in the late 1880s, and the price of the Moore property followed in step. Amazingly, just nine years after it sold for $10,000, the property was given away for "Love and Affection." One month later, the property sold for $10. In 1903, the ten-acre Moore Vineyard was acquired by merchant seaman Pleasant Ashley

Stevens and is recognized as one of the oldest vineyards in Napa Valley and one of the top sources for old-vine Zinfandel in California. Pleasant was a colorful character who, with the help of his daughters, planted St. George roots and grafted them to Zinfandel.

In 1983, an orthodontist named Bill Moore purchased the vineyard and over the ensuing years has lovingly preserved and restored it. Like many old Zinfandel vineyards, the Moore vineyard has small quantities of other varietals interplanted with the Zinfandel. These include Carignane, Mourvedre, Petite Sirah and Napa Gamay. These varietals represent less than 5 percent of the total. Current winemakers using grapes from the R.W. Moore Vineyard include Mike and Molly Hendry and Robert Biale Vineyards.

Sonoma County also has its share of historic vineyards. William McPherson Hill founded Old Hill Ranch in 1851. Hill is believed to be the first grower in Sonoma to plant nonmission grape varieties, which he imported from Peru. Hill was born in Hatboro, Pennsylvania, on October 22, 1822, and ventured west to California with his father, Dr. John D. Hill. The Hills arrived in San Francisco in 1849 and lived there for two years. They were engaged in the lumber and mining enterprises there. In 1851, they headed for Sonoma, where they purchased land and planted fruit trees and grapevines. Hill's father became a California state senator in 1861 and served consecutively, except for one term, and was succeeded by his son, William. John Hill lived to be ninety-two years old.

As early as 1855, when Hill and General Vallejo owned the most extensive vineyards in Sonoma County, Hill is thought to have already planted Zinfandel. By 1860, Hill, his wife, Annie Elmer Potter-Hill, and their son, Robert, were residing with Hill's father, John, on the land the two men purchased. Ten years later saw the Hills with more children, including Robert, Howard and Eliza. William's brother, Humphrey, was also residing with them, as were four Chinese immigrants and an Irish lass named Mary Collins, all of whom worked for the Hills.

In December 1871, the *Pacific Rural Press* noted, "We sampled a bottle of wine from the cellar of Wm. McPherson Hill made from the Zinfandel grape, a new variety that is growing in favor with winemakers. The wine was pronounced by the gentlemen who tasted it to be superior to any they had seen in the state." In 1877, Hill was a state senator representing Napa, Lake and Sonoma Counties. A writer named R.R. Parkinson wrote an article on California senators called "Pen Portraits." In it, he described Hill as *a Democrat to the backbone, and by occupation and profession a general farmer, with the culture of the grapevine as his specialty. He is a native of Pennsylvania, and came to California in 1849, via Cape Horn, and was 202 days in making the voyage. Mr. Hill is one of Sonoma's most prominent and honored citizens, has been one of its Supervisors for three years, and President of the Sonoma County Agricultural Society. He has also filled the position of President of the San Pablo District Pioneer Society for two years. Mr. Hill is now serving the second session of his term, which will expire December 1879. He is a dignified and social gentleman, and at the last session of the Legislature, by his consistent and manly course, gained the approbation and confidence of his constituents, and the esteem of his fellow-Senators. His watchword is, "economy and retrenchment in the government of the State," and his votes of the present session stand a living monument to his credit, that his practices are consistent with his teachings. He is an able Senator well posted on matters of legislation, and advocates what he concedes to be right, regardless of anybody or anything else. He never bores the Senate with long speeches, but says that he means in a plain, comprehensive manner, and when he is done, and he quits. Mr. Hill is chairman of Committee on Agriculture, and a member of Committee on Counties and County Boundaries, Roads and Highways, State Prison, and Fisheries and Game.*

On December 12, 1889, Hill sold 1,600 acres to the State of California so a home for "feeble-minded" children could be built. Today, it's the Sonoma Developmental Center. While Hill sold much of his land, he kept two parcels—the southeast corner 60-acre portion, which is now Old Hill Ranch, and a 100-acre parcel on Sonoma Mountain that son Robert sold to Jack London in 1903. Upon Hill's death on November 19, 1897, the land was passed on to his son, Robert Potter Hill, who farmed the ranch until his demise in 1940.

Otto and Anne Teller purchased Old Hill Ranch in 1981. The previous owners had not set foot on the property since their house, the original Hill House, burned down several years earlier. The overgrown vineyard was barely visible beneath the blackberry vines and poison oak. A UC-Davis farm advisor took one look and strongly recommended ripping up the vineyard and starting fresh. This was not the answer that Otto was seeking, so he turned to one of the few winemakers in the area who understood the value of old vines, Joel Peterson at Ravenswood Winery. Joel recommended selling the grapes to Ravenswood, and so Otto began the long process of bringing the vineyard back to health. In 1983, Ravenswood began its vineyard designate Old Hill Ranch Zinfandel just as the vineyard was turning one hundred years old. You can still taste wine made from these historic grapes from the Bucklin Winery. Its Zinfandel is produced from a certified organic, dry-farmed field blend planted on Old Hill in the 1880s. It's called Old Hill Ranch Zinfandel (Ancient Vine). Ravenswood Winery also makes an old Hill Vineyard Designate.

Morgan Peterson, son of Joel Peterson of Ravenswood fame, is the caretaker for several old vineyards in the Sonoma Valley. The Bedrock Vineyard, which contains 152 acres in the heart of Sonoma Valley, was founded in 1854 by General William Tecumseh Sherman and General "Fightin' Joe" Hooker. Following the first epidemic of phylloxera in the mid-1880s, the vineyard was replanted in 1888 by Senator George Hearst. (See page 73 for more on this.) It is from those 120-year-old vines that the Bedrock Heirloom Wine is crafted.

In 1934, the property was purchased by the Parducci family and was part of the estate vineyards of early Valley of the Moon Winery.

The Stellwagen Vineyard is only one mile away from Bedrock Vineyard in the heart of the Sonoma Valley. Morgan Peterson wrote, "It is almost as old—I suspect the vineyard was once part of the old Steiger property, probably planted in the 1890s. Though geographically close, Stellwagen lies on a soil type unseen on our ranch—Los Robles Cobbly Loams. This is a darker, more gravelly, soil also found at nearby Old Hill Ranch. The vineyard is owned by Ruth Stellwagen and her husband Robert—longtime valley folk, and part of the family that has owned Stellwagen since the 1960s." He used grapes from the vineyard to make wine at his Bedrock Wine Company.

Also managed by Morgan Peterson is the Saitone Ranch, which, Peterson wrote, "is the oldest remaining vineyard in the Piner-Olivet area of the Russian River Valley. Located next to Papera Ranch, Saitone was planted in 1896 and features a diverse array of interplanted varieties of both red and white hue. It is a thrill to be working with the legendary Ulises Valdez who has taken over the farming of the vineyard starting with vintage 2011. Unlike the neighboring Papera, where Bedrock Wine Company will make a field-blended Heirloom wine that will be roughly 50% Zinfandel, the Saitone Ranch will be a Zinfandel."

The Saxon-Brown and Mayo families are credited with planting the Casa Santinamaria Vineyard. Morgan Peterson wrote:

Planted in 1905, [it] is probably the coolest Zinfandel site Bedrock Wine Company works with in Sonoma Valley. Located behind the old Casa, which at one time was a local church and still possesses the bell-tower, at the intersection of Boyes Boulevard and Arnold Drive, the vineyard is composed of both old-vine Zinfandel and mixed blacks, along with two blocks of field-blended white grapes. Half of this vineyard was split of several decades ago and subdivided. Those vines have long gone to Rosenblum Winery for their famous Maggie's Reserve. Also, the field-blended Semillon, Muscadelle, Chasselas, and Palomino, will find their way into the Cuvee Caritas and perhaps even into an Heirloom White wine from the vineyard. It is a thrill to be working with such a gorgeous piece of land!

Sometime before 1892, the Barricia Vineyard was planted, and today it contains six acres of Zinfandel. The land dates back to General Mariano Vallejo, who traded it to his children's music teacher in exchange for lessons. In 1978, Barbara Olesen and Patricia Herron bought the vineyard and named it Barricia by combining their own first names. In 2006, Pat decided to sell the winery since she was now alone after Barbara passed away and also because she had turned eighty. Mel and Angela Dagovich bought the vineyard and still own it today. Joel Peterson from Ravenswood Winery makes a Barricia Zinfandel with their grapes.

At the urging of his fellow Hungarian Agoston Haraszthy, Louis Csomortanyi planted forty acres in Sonoma in 1860. Csomortanyi also built a small cottage and stone winey. In 1873, the property was purchased by longtime vintners and wine merchants Charles Kohler and John Frohling. They expanded the vineyards to more than two hundred acres and built a large winery capable of producing more than sixty thousand cases per year. Despite having Kohler and Frohling at the helm, the winery's production declined, and the 1906 earthquake damaged it beyond practical repair.

Enter author Jack London. He first came to the valley to court Charmian Kittredge, and after they were married in 1905, he purchased the beautiful Hill Ranch, where his dream home, the Wolf House, was built. He wrote, "There are 130 acres in the place, and they are 130 acres of the most beautiful, primitive land to be found in California." Over the next eight years, London purchased six adjacent properties to create his 1,400-acre Beauty Ranch. Carefully terraced under London's supervision, the ranch produced grapes and hay and provided an inspiring view from his writing den in the cottage that became the couple's home in 1911. Several of the author's later books were written at Beauty Ranch, including *Burning Daylight* and *The Valley of the Moon*.

During London's frequent travels, his stepsister, Eliza Shepard, managed Beauty Ranch. Upon his untimely death in 1916 at age forty, she took over management full time. The vineyard and hayfield were left fallow due to World War I and the advent of prohibition, but Shepard and her descendants kept Beauty Ranch largely intact until 1959, four years after Charmian London's death, when the family donated land for the establishment of Jack London State Park.

In 1972, Eliza Shepard's son, Irving, who had taken over responsibility for the ranch upon her death, and his son, Milo, planted Jack London Vineyard, which remains under family ownership. A substantial percentage of the vineyard was established on the old terraces that London built. The superb quality of the first Cabernet Sauvignon vintage motivated neighboring Kenwood Vineyards to enter an exclusive agreement to purchase the grapes from Jack London Vineyard. Jack London Cabernet Sauvignon, with a label featuring London's "Wolf" bookplate logo, debuted with the 1977 vintage. Kenwood Vineyards has been producing wines made exclusively from the Jack London Vineyard for more than thirty years.

Felice Pagani was born in 1863 in Fenegrò, Italy, and was one of twelve children. Fenegrò was a tiny, poor village close to the border of Switzerland. Most residents labored in the local silk factory, described as "cold, wet, and miserable" by Norma, Felice's granddaughter. At age twenty, hoping to improve his prospects, Felice immigrated to the United States. He spent two years in Vermont felling trees until the cold weather drove him to Sonoma Valley in the 1880s, and he found work there at the Goldstein Ranch in Glen Ellen. Before long, the hardworking Felice "became foreman of Goldstein's vineyards. Today the property, known as Monte Rosso Vineyard, now owned by Louis M. Martini, is famed for its old-vine Zinfandel, which was tended by Felice" when both he and the vines were young.

Sometime around 1890, Felice sent back to Italy for sixteen-year-old Angela Bogani to become his wife. "The last time he'd seen Angela she was probably eight or nine," Norma said. "But he knew she came from a good family." Norma's sister, Charlotte Pagani-Savinovich, said, "He'd liked her older sister…She was pretty and fun. He figured Angela would be a lot like her." At first, the couple lived on the Goldstein Ranch. Angela soon gave birth to their first child, Rose, followed by Charles, who would grow up to

Louis Pagani, riding his new tractor in 1926. *Courtesy of the Pagani family and Dino Amantite.*

be the father of Norma, Charlotte and their sister, Marie Pagani-Meursinge. Felice and Angela ultimately had seven children, although only four lived past childhood.

Felice sometimes brought his crew down the hill to work twenty-five acres of vines planted in the early 1880s—mostly Zinfandel with a classic field blend of varietals that included Petite Sirah, Alicante, Grand Noir and Lenoir—on land belonging to Judge Cook. In 1903, Cook sold the land, today's "lower ranch," to Pagani. The Pagani farm was typical for the day. "They grew everything," says great-grandson Dino Amantite. "You name it: grapes, prunes, apples, pears, cattle, silage and hay, chickens and pigs. They had horses and plowed with them. It wasn't until after Felice died that they bought a tractor." Shortly before the 1906 earthquake, Felice built a two-story wooden barn. One wall had to be rebuilt after the quake, but the barn is still used today.

In 1913, the family also bought a sawmill and stone winery (today's Jack London Village) from Henry Chauvet. They started the A. Pagani Winery, which lasted until 1969. "They had the first label that said Glen Ellen winery," said Dino. "There was a tasting room when I was a kid. It was very informal, and they'd take it right out of the barrel. They also made brandy there." In 1919, Felice bought an adjoining property, today's "upper ranch," planting it in 1921 and 1922 with thirty acres of vines. When Felice died in

1926, three of his children—Charles, Louis and Olive—took over the ranch. After Charles's death in 1954, "the shots were called by Uncle Louie and Olive," Dino said.

Charles's daughters married and moved from Glen Ellen with their husbands, returning to help out when they could. The only one who yearned to return to the ranch for good was Norma, who lived in Point Richmond with her husband and three sons. "I always came up to help out at harvest," Norma said. "I kept hoping they'd ask me to move up. But it wasn't until 1972 that Louie, by then in his seventies, felt that he needed help. Uncle Louie asked me to move to the ranch. I said, 'I've been waiting 17½ years for that offer.'" Asked what she might say to Felice if she could, Norma responded simply, "I'd just thank him for buying this property."

Today, the Pagani Ranch is run by the third and fourth generation, with Norma as ranch manager and Dino managing the vineyard. Wineries currently making wine from the Pagani Ranch include Seghesio Family Vineyards, Ridge Vineyards, Bedrock Wine Company, Robert Biale Vineyards, Wellington Vineyards and Berthoud Vineyards and Winery.

Acorn Winery's Alegria Vineyard in Healdsburg traces its history back to George Brumfield, who came from Virginia in 1852. But before Brumfield bought it, the vineyard was part of the 1841 Sotoyome land grant from Mexican governor Micheltorena to Captain Henry Delano Fitch. Fitch was native of New Hampshire who married Josefa Carrillo, sister-in-law of General Mariano Vallejo. Fitch had come to the area in about 1833. George Brumfield and his family, who migrated from Virginia, settled on the land in 1852. Like all of the residents of the Healdsburg area at that time, they were squatters on Fitch's land and did not get title until 1857.

Their 850-acre property also included the present Ponzo Vineyards. George Brumfield transferred the property to his son, Summers Brumfield, in 1867. The California Board of State Viticultural Commissioners' 1891 *Directory of Grape Growers* shows Summers Brumfield as having 18 acres of Zinfandel and mission grapes in 1889, producing 1.67 tons/acre, which would indicate planting in 1886 or earlier, but those vines were probably not on phylloxera-resistant rootstock. Brumfield sold 85 acres, including Alegria, in 1895 to George Davis, who sold the vineyard in 1896 to Elizabeth Moes. Moes got the western half of the Davis parcel; the eastern half later became the Pedroncelli Winery, which is no longer there. Moes built a small winery on her property, and when she died in 1924, her daughter, Ernestine, and son-in-law, Adolph DiNucci, maintained the vineyard during prohibition and until 1943. The vineyard then passed through a series of owners, including Reynaud, Pavone, Mericone and Mohr. It was then purchased in 1947 by Americo Rafanelli, who replanted part of the vineyard in 1950. Rafanelli sold in 1951 to Arnold Bruschera, who sold in 1973 to the Allens, who sold to Betsy and Bill Nachbaur in 1990.

You can experience the varied history with the Heritage Vines Zinfandel, which are blocks of a mixed planting that include Zinfandel, Petite Sirah and Alicante Bouschet. The remaining includes Carignane, Trousseau, Sangiovese, Petit Bouschet, Negrette, Syrah, Plavac Mali, Tannat, Muscat Noir, Peloursin, Beclan, Mataro, Cinsaut, Grenache and a few white grapes of Palomino and Monbadon. The unique blend of interplanted varieties evolved over the years; as a vine died, it was replaced, but not necessarily with the same variety. Today, Acorn Winery, DeLoach Vineyards and Rock Wall Wine Company all make wine with the Alegria Vineyard grapes.

Chapter 6

TWO DEADLY "P" WORDS

Phylloxera and Prohibition

The first of the two noxious words is "phylloxera," which came about for the first time in California's vineyards during the mid- to late 1800s. This grapevine pest is a root louse insect that attacks the root system; this slowly kills the vines, thus killing the grapes and any potential wine. It's very likely that the pest was there earlier, but it had yet to be identified as phylloxera. It was detected in Sonoma during the 1870s by the Buena Vista Vinicultural Society, which had already lost some one hundred acres of vines.

The *San Francisco Bulletin* printed a story about phylloxera on June 17, 1873, stating, "The insect which has been so destructive to the vineyards of Europe, has been known in the United States for some time. We learn from vinticulturists of long experience that it has been found in various parts of California, it having come in, as is supposed, with grape cuttings. It is very destructive when once it has possession of a vineyard." It also reprinted a letter that well-known winemakers Charles Kohler and John Frohling wrote to the Department of Agriculture in Washington, D.C. They asked that imported vines be restricted, similar to what the German government did to stop the importation of vines from Los Angeles and Sonoma. Commissioner Frederick Watts replied, "[W]hile this insect has been known to exist in the United States for many years, its ravages have not been of a character to seriously alarm grape growers."

Because of reports like those, many thought that phylloxera would not affect California vineyards like it had done in France and other European countries in the late 1880s. However, the widespread infestation became unmistakable in the 1880s. Gulian Rixford was a member of the California State Horticultural Society in San Francisco, and in 1880, he sent samples of his vines from the Fresno area, which was thought to be infected with "Grapevine Krat." The California State Horticultural Society asked Justin P. Moore to make a presentation at its May 1880 meeting. Moore described it as a "disease…[that] attacks the roots as well as the young shoots." It sounds like they were describing phylloxera but did not know it. It was first believed that the bugs were from vines imported from France, but it was later discovered that the disease actually originated in the United States.

During the last quarter of the nineteenth century, Napa Valley was a thriving viticultural community with nearly 140 wineries. However, in the late 1890s, phylloxera brought wine production in Napa and other areas to a standstill. The solution to the phylloxera problem was, and still is, to first plant resistant rootstocks and then graft grape varietals to the roots. Records of using this approach in California were documented as early as 1896. Sacramento's *Record-Union* ran a story on December 4, 1896, on recent findings from the University of California's Agricultural Experiment Station. It reported:

> *Following is the full text of Bulletin No. 12 just issued by E.J. Wickson, Associate Professor of Agriculture…*SELECTED RESISTANT VINES. *It has been known for years that American wild wines are characterized by very marked differences in degrees of resistance to phylloxera and especially in adaptability to soils…of the few varieties which have this demonstrated particular excellence in France we have obtained stock of four varieties which promise best under California conditions. First, for dry soils—that is, soils likely to become somewhat dry in summer—the Rupestris "St. George." It must be understood that the vines do not grow edible grapes; they are merely intended for roots on which to graft the desirable table and wine varieties.*

They went on to state that they would distribute their vines and cuttings equally between any applicants desiring them. They asked applicants to describe their soil and vineyards and send along twenty-five cents for postage and packaging so that they could best determine which vines to send. However, vineyardists had already begun using rootstock like Lenoir in the 1880s.

Phylloxera finished gorging itself on more than 100,000 acres of California vineyards, Rupestris St. George was grafted and wine production began once again. Flourishing for about forty years, California produced some promising wines, and California winemakers were optimistic about the future of their wines. After growers and winemakers soon recovered with replanted vines, they were hit with another setback. Prohibition was ratified in 1919 and went into effect in 1920, and once again California's wine industry suffered—as did the nation.

Enter the second deadly "p" word. On January 16, 1919, the Eighteenth Amendment was ratified, and one year later, alcohol was illegal. The Volstead Act was required legislation that enabled the government to enforce the amendment and was formally known as the National Prohibition Act. The term "prohibition" was all encompassing in the Eighteenth Amendment and its supporting legislation. Pioneer J.A. Graves recalled, "Just when this industry was at the peak of its importance, the Eighteenth Amendment to the Constitution was passed, and while it is by no means enforced under the Volstead Act, it has certainly crippled an industry that brought great wealth and an excellent reputation to the Golden State."

The Eighteenth Amendment began: "Section 1. After one year from the ratification of this article the manufacture, sale, or transportation of intoxicating liquors within, the importation thereof into, or the exportation thereof from the United States and all territory subject to the jurisdiction thereof for beverage purposes is hereby prohibited." While the Eighteenth Amendment established prohibition, it was the Volstead Act (passed on October 28, 1919) that clarified the law.

Title I, Section 1 of the Volstead Act stated, "The words beer, wine, or other intoxicating malt or vinous liquors in the War Prohibition Act shall be hereafter construed to mean any such beverages which contain one-half of 1 per centum or more of alcoholic beverages by volume." It seems that even some of the Volstead Act writers didn't approve of the act because it contained loopholes. For example, Title II, Section 3 addressed the use of alcohol for religious reasons: "Liquor for non-beverage purposes and wine for sacramental purposes may be manufactured, purchased, sold, bartered, transported, imported, exported, delivered furnished and possessed, but only as herein provided, and the commissioner may, upon application, issue permits therefor."

Section 6 addressed using alcohol for medicinal reasons: "[E]xcept that a person may, without a permit, purchase and use liquor for medicinal purposes when prescribed by a physician as herein provided, and except that any person who in the opinion of the commissioner is conducting a bona fide hospital or sanatorium engaged in the treatment of persons suffering from alcoholism, may, under such rules, regulations, and conditions as the commissioner shall prescribe, purchase and use, in accordance with the methods in use in such institution, liquor, to be administered to the patients of such institution under the direction of a duly qualified physician employed by such institution."

Section 29 of the Act stated, "The penalties provided in this Act against the manufacture of liquor without a permit shall not apply to a person for manufacturing non-intoxicating cider and fruit juices exclusively for use in his home, but such cider and fruit juices shall not be sold or delivered except to persons having permits to manufacture vinegar." Title II, Section I defined what exactly was considered illegal: "[T]he word 'liquor' or the phrase 'intoxicating liquor' shall be construed to include alcohol, brandy, whisky, rum, gin, beer, ale, porter, and wine, and in addition thereto any spirituous, vinous, malt, or fermented liquor, liquids, and compounds, whether medicated, proprietary, patented, or not, and by whatever name called, containing one-half of 1 per centum or more of alcohol by volume which are fit for use for beverage purposes."

Despite some loopholes, the National Prohibition Act nearly ended California's wine industry, and many winemakers and grape growers didn't survive the thirteen-year dry spell. Others did manage to make it and survived by growing their grapes under Section 3 by manufacturing, purchasing and selling "non-beverage wine," or sacramental wines. Only a handful of wineries were allowed to sell sacramental wine; there were hundreds of thousands of religious conversions all across America. Some also turned their Zinfandel, mission, Riesling and Burgundy grapes into grape juice.

Products like concentrated grape juice and concentrated grape bricks were other ways that desperate winemakers and grape growers got around prohibition under Section 29. It allowed them to legally ship unfermented grape juice in products called Virginia Dare Tonic, Vine-Glo and Vino Sano. Grape growers included a packet of yeast and advised buyers to be wary of adding it and letting the bottle sit at a certain temperature…or it would turn to alcohol. Vino Sano advertised, "A juice compound to produce the following flavors: grape, orange, lemon, Port, Sherry, Burgundy, Tokay, Champagne, Muscatel, Rhine. Do not consume within 5 days. Caution: This juice may ferment and make wine." One has to wonder how many people "accidentally" made wine.

Louis J. Foppiano of Foppiano Vineyards recalled the Alicante grape and prohibition in a 1996 interview: "We had some. We planted in when Prohibition came in because that was the grape that the New York people wanted to buy because it had color. They'd ferment it, draw the wine off

Harvesting sacramental and medicinal grapes during prohibition in 1923. *Courtesy of Library of Congress.*

it, and then they'd put sugar and water back in and ferment it again and make more wine…It wasn't good wine, but they drank it and sold it. These families would sell it to their neighbors or some speakeasy."

On December 5, 1933, Utah became the final state needed for a three-quarter majority and ratified the Twenty-first Amendment. While the amendment still allowed for state and local levels of prohibition, by 1966 there were no state laws banning alcohol.

The 1933 repeal found California's wine industry decimated. Production had fallen more than 90 percent, and fewer than two hundred of California's original seven hundred wineries were still in existence. The resiliency of California winemakers was evident as pioneers and newcomers alike began rebuilding their businesses. Today, California has a thriving wine industry due to the pioneering spirit of both old and new winemakers and grape growers.

BIBLIOGRAPHY

Beer, Jeremy. *Organically Sublime, Sustainably Ridiculous: The first Quarter-Century of Frog's Leap.* Kennett Square, PA: Union Street Press, 2007.

Bioletti, Frederic T. *Protection of Vineyards from Phylloxera.* Berkeley: University of California, College of Agriculture, Agricultural Experiment Station, 1920.

California Farmer and Journal of Useful Sciences. June 1, 1860.

De Turk, Isaac. *The Vineyards in Sonoma County.* Sacramento: California Board of State Viticultural Commissioners, 1893.

Funding Universe. "F. Korbel & Bros. Inc. History." www.fundinguniverse. com/company-histories/f-korbel-bros-inc-history.

Graves, J.A. *My Seventy Years in California, 1857–1927.* Los Angeles, CA: Times-Mirror Press, 1927.

Guinn, J.M. *History of the State of California.* Chicago: Chapman Publishing Group, 1904.

Heintz, William F. *A Brief Glimpse into the History of the Charles Krug Winery.* Sonoma, CA: privately published, 1984.

———. *A Brief Glimpse into the History of Wildwood Winery & Vineyards.* Sonoma, CA: privately published, 1984.

———. *Researching the History of the Kunde Vineyards.* Sonoma, CA: privately published, 1990.

Leach, Frank. *Recollections of a Newspaperman: A Record of Life and Events in California.* San Francisco, CA: A.S. Levinson, 1917.

Menefee, Campbell Augustus. *Historical and Descriptive Sketch Book of Napa, Sonoma, Lake and Mendocino.* Napa City, CA: Reporter Publishing House, 1873.

Napa Journal. July 15, 1888. Author's collection.

Pagani family history. E-mail correspondence with author.

Purdy, Tim I. *Lassen County Almanac: An Historical Encyclopedia.* Susanville, CA Lahontan Images, 2002.

Rixford, Emmett H. *The Wine Press and the Cellar.* San Francisco, CA: Payot, Upham & Company, 1883.

Wait, Frona Eunice. *Wines & Vines of California.* San Francisco, CA: Bancroft Company, 1889.

White, Katherine A., *California as I Saw It: First-Person Narratives of California's Early Years, 1849–1900.* "A Yankee Trader in the Gold Rush; The Letters of Franklin A. Buck." Library of Congress, General Collections.

INDEX

ABOUT THE AUTHOR

Sherry Monahan is the vice-president (2012–14) of Western Writers of America and the author of several books on the Victorian West, including *Taste of Tombstone*, *The Wicked West: Boozers, Cruisers, Gamblers, and More* and *Tombstone's Treasure: Silver Mines & Golden Saloons*. Sherry also writes a "Frontier Fare" column for *True West* magazine and works as a marketing consultant and professional genealogist. As the "Genie with a Bottle," she traces the genealogy of food and wine. She calls it "Winestry" and says, "History never tasted so good."